RAND PROJECT AIR FORCE

T0131039

Attracting, Recruiting, and Retaining Successful Cyberspace Operations Officers

Cyber Workforce Interview Findings

Chaitra M. Hardison, Leslie Adrienne Payne, John A. Hamm, Angela Clague, Jacqueline Torres, David Schulker, John S. Crown

Prepared for the United States Air Force

Approved for public release; distribution unlimited

For more information on this publication, visit www.rand.org/t/RR2618

Library of Congress Cataloging-in-Publication Data is available for this publication.
ISBN: 978-1-9774-0101-4

Published by the RAND Corporation, Santa Monica, Calif.
© Copyright 2019 RAND Corporation
RAND® is a registered trademark.

Support RAND
Make a tax-deductible charitable contribution at
www.rand.org/giving/contribute

www.rand.org

Preface

Cybersecurity is one of the most serious economic and national security challenges we face as a nation. Given the U.S. Air Force mission to "fly, fight and win in air, space and cyberspace," addressing this potential security threat falls squarely within the Air Force's responsibility. Because of concerns over the current health and future state of the Air Force's cyberspace community, Air Force leadership asked RAND Project AIR FORCE (PAF) to explore perspectives within the cyberspace operations officer (17D) community to help the Air Force gain insights into key drivers of retention and attraction to the career field.

PAF has pursued several lines of research. First, we explored what is already known about the issues within the 17D community, which included a review of relevant literature. Second, we analyzed Air Force personnel data files to better understand key characteristics of the Air Force's cyber workforce. Third, we conducted a series of interviews with three key populations—senior subject matter experts (SMEs) within the 17D community, members of the 17D workforce, and private-sector cyber specialists. The insights gained from these discussions informed our findings and recommendations, which are detailed in this report. Human subjects protection protocols were used in this study in accordance with the appropriate statutes and Department of Defense (DoD) regulations governing human subjects protection. The views of the sources quoted in this report—including those who have not been identified—are solely their own and do not represent the official policy or position of the DoD or the U.S. Government.

The research reported here was sponsored by Maj Gen Patrick C. Higby (SAF/CIO A6S), director of cyberspace strategy and policy for the Office of Information Dominance and chief information officer for the Office of the Secretary of the Air Force, and conducted within the Manpower, Personnel, and Training Program of RAND PAF as part of the FY 2017 project Attracting and Retaining Cyber Professionals, and Fostering Their Success in the Air Force.

RAND Project AIR FORCE

RAND Project AIR FORCE (PAF), a division of the RAND Corporation, is the U.S. Air Force's federally funded research and development center for studies and analyses. PAF provides the Air Force with independent analyses of policy alternatives affecting the development, employment, combat readiness, and support of current and future air, space, and cyber forces. Research is conducted in four programs: Force Modernization and Employment; Manpower, Personnel, and Training; Resource Management; and Strategy and Doctrine. The research reported here was prepared under contract FA7014-16-D-1000.

Additional information about PAF is available on our website: http://www.rand.org/paf/
This report documents work originally shared with the U.S. Air Force on October 26, 2017.
The draft report, issued on February 12, 2018, was reviewed by formal peer reviewers and
U.S. Air Force subject-matter experts.

Contents

Figures

Tables

Summary

Cybersecurity is one of the most serious security challenges we face as a nation. This is reflected clearly in the Air Force's mission to "fly, fight and win in air, space and cyberspace." While there are many factors that ultimately contribute to mission success in cyberspace, one area that directly impacts the Air Force's ability to defeat its cyber adversaries is the quality and readiness of its workforce. Yet many are concerned with the current health and future state of the Air Force's cyberspace workforce.

The Air Force has acknowledged that it is facing a large shortage of field grade cyber officers, in the near and long term, raising concerns about retention now and in the future.[1] The fact that demand for skilled Air Force cyber officers in both the Air Force and joint community is high only exacerbates that concern. In addition, the Air Force may face stiff competition with the private sector in attracting and retaining top cyber talent that could make it difficult to build and maintain a highly capable cyber workforce. Finally, because some airmen in the cyber field receive extensive highly technical training from the Air Force that further increases their marketability, the Air Force is concerned that it may lose talented personnel to competition with the private sector.

Because of anticipated challenges in recruiting and retaining a high-quality cyber workforce in both the near and long term, Air Force leadership asked RAND Project AIR FORCE (PAF) to explore perspectives within the cyberspace operations officer (17D) career field on the major drivers of attraction to and retention in the career field and to recommend ideas for initiatives to help identify, recruit, and retain successful cyber personnel.

Approach

To help the Air Force gain insights into key drivers for attracting and retaining officers into the cyber operations career field and essential characteristics of high-performing cyber personnel, we pursued several lines of research:

- We reviewed what is already known about the issues facing the 17D career field. We talked with a range of cyber officer subject matter experts (SMEs) and reviewed research on the cyber workforce in the Air Force and the private sector. This research informed our discussions with a wide cross-section of individuals in the Air Force cyber community and select individuals in the private sector.
- We explored Air Force personnel data files to better understand key characteristics of the Air Force cyber workforce.

---

[1] We use *cyber officer* and *cyberspace operations officer* interchangeably throughout this report.

- We conducted a series of group and/or individual interviews with three key populations: (1) SMEs at the lieutenant colonel, colonel, and general officer levels within the 17D community; (2) officers in the 17D workforce at the grade of lieutenant colonel and below; and (3) private-sector cyber specialists.
- As part of the focus group discussions with officers in the cyber workforce, we administered a questionnaire to participants that asked about their satisfaction with various aspects of the career field and their views on knowledge, skills, and attributes needed within in the community.

Knowledge, Skills, and Abilities of a High-Quality Cyber Officer

If the Air Force aims to attract, develop, and retain the highest-quality cyber workforce, it needs to first clearly define the knowledge, skills, abilities, and other characteristics (KSAOs) that lead to cyber mission success. To help define those characteristics, we reviewed existing research literature defining those KSAOs and asked our SMEs and 17D workforce participants for their thoughts on the KSAOs that are important for cyber officers to possess.

Our review of recent research literature identified a number of important KSAOs desired in cyber personnel that may be of interest to the Air Force. However, because the cyber domain encompasses many different functions and is rapidly evolving, it can be difficult to form a clear picture of the type of professional that might epitomize a successful cyber operator in all contexts (National Research Council, 2013). Also recognizing that the qualities needed in the Air Force may differ in meaningful ways from those needed in the private sector, we sought views on this topic from SMEs and members of the 17D workforce within the Air Force.

Synthesizing the KSAOs from the existing studies of the cyber workforce field, one can see the beginnings of a coherent picture of a successful cyberspace professional. For example, successful cybersecurity professionals need technical knowledge of computers and networks, but they also need knowledge in auxiliary areas such a legal and regulatory policy. Necessary skills include forensic analysis—that is, finding and eliminating threats and vulnerabilities—but also the ability to design robust and secure information technology (IT) systems. The ideal cybersecurity operator would possess a distinct set of cognitive abilities, but also noncognitive traits such as intense curiosity that might drive him or her to operate at the high level needed to counter the most sophisticated cyber adversaries. Many of the KSAOs identified in the literature for IT support and maintenance roles overlap with those needed in cybersecurity.

When we asked SMEs and 17D officers in the cyber workforce more specifically about the skills needed for ensuring mission success within the 17D community, we learned the following:

- KSAOs identified by our SMEs were similar to those identified by members of the 17D workforce. They included technical aptitude and critical thinking, leadership skills, and the "warfighting mind-set."
- Members of the 17D workforce also mentioned having a strategic and operational understanding of the bigger picture and being good at communicating with various stakeholders as critically important. Extended discussion took place on this topic because

many respondents believed the community was particularly weak in these areas and in need of improvement.

- SMEs and members of the 17D workforce both provided mixed responses on whether a degree in the fields of science, technology, engineering, and mathematics (STEM) is preferable. Those in favor of being open-minded about academic background felt that different degrees offer varying perspectives that can be valuable.

Improving the nation's cybersecurity has received a great deal of policy emphasis and study in the wake of several high-profile and costly attacks. Yet, the KSAOs that cybersecurity and IT professionals need in order to improve security are not so well defined that wide standardization and formal academic training can meet cybersecurity and IT demands. This puts the 17D career field in a position where it must chart its own course to providing cyber capabilities (in conjunction with national security partners) by attracting raw talent and continually investing in job satisfaction and skill development. As suggested here, an ideal cyber operator likely possesses a mix of technical and managerial skills, as well as noncognitive traits (such as creativity). The task of career field planners, then, will be to determine a strategy for which characteristics should be part of recruiting (i.e., screening), and which should be part of training and development. Further, such a strategy also needs to retain sufficient numbers of operators with the right skills to sustain the career field. Long-term mission success requires no less than successful recruiting, development, and retention of officers with those traits.

That said, it is also important to note that the characteristics of successful cyber operators identified in this study and elsewhere are based largely on perceptions of cyber SMEs and job incumbents. While those perceptions are a good starting point for answering the question of what KSAOs are needed, more certainly could be done. Very little research has been done linking those KSAOs to actual performance of cyber operators (and, in this case, cyber officers) on the job. As such, collecting data on that performance and further exploring the relevant KSAOs related to it in future studies would be worthwhile.

Key Findings Regarding Sources of Dissatisfaction Within the Workforce

In addition to asking our SMEs and 17D workforce participants about the KSAOs needed in the career field, we also asked them about their views on the major sources of dissatisfaction and drivers of attraction to and retention with the community.

Our discussions with these participants yielded a number of interesting findings about sources of satisfaction and dissatisfaction within the career field, many of which they also speculated were drivers of attraction and retention. The following are areas they discussed frequently:

- Many want to be able to do technical work for longer in their career.
- A perceived lack of clarity in the vision for the cyber workforce is hindering the mission and morale. Little connection is made between strategic vision and the tactical task on which the workforce focuses on a day-to-day basis.

- Assignments to cyberwarfare operations (17S) positions are typically viewed as more attractive, but few such assignments are available, leading to widespread disappointment.
- Retention of personnel with 17S experience may be a concern, especially if they fear being shifted away from 17S assignments when their service commitment is up.
- There is a perceived mismatch between the training provided and (1) the skill levels of people completing it; (2) the type of work people will be doing (information network support versus offensive cyber operations versus defensive cyber operations); and (3) the practical day-to-day procedural information needed in the field.
- Critical technical acumen may be atrophying as a result of not allowing cyberspace professionals to stay in technical roles or not providing adequate continuation training during their careers.
- Some do not feel as though the cyber mission is adequately resourced; this includes resourcing manning, training, simulators, and cybertechnology.
- The Air Force's acquisition and decisionmaking processes are not agile enough to address the cyber enterprise's needs.

That said, a note of caution in interpreting these findings is warranted. Although these were themes that were mentioned as sources of dissatisfaction by multiple groups and individuals within the community, it is important to remember that the results presented in this chapter only give us insights into people's perceptions on these issues. These perceptions may or may not be grounded in reality. For example, it is possible that the Air Force's acquisition process is very agile, flexible, and responsive to the cyber community's needs, despite a perception that exists to the contrary. For that reason, more research may be needed to explore the veracity of the community's views on some of these issues, and to the extent that leadership questions whether certain beliefs are true (e.g., whether training is poor, acquisition lacks needed agility, resources are inadequate, etc.), additional research that tests out the premises behind these concerns should be pursued.

Nevertheless, these are the views held by the people we talked with, regardless of whether there is truth in those views. It is therefore also important to point out that the existence of a shared negative perception or shared concerns in a workforce ought not to be ignored for two reasons: first, they may signal that in fact there may be truth in the matter (e.g., perhaps agility in the acquisition process is a real problem); and second, perceptions matter because they influence people's behavior. That is, if personnel perceive a problem (even if, in fact, there is no such problem), it can still lead to dissatisfaction and other negative outcomes, including attrition. For that reason, taking action to either fix a problem or change the perception that there is a problem is a critical step in combating any problems with retention or interest in the career field.

Recommendations

Taken as a whole, our research efforts suggest a number of changes that cyber leadership should consider making in managing the cyber enterprise and the career field. It is important to note again, however, that the changes we suggest are based entirely on people's perceptions of problems within the community. In the absence of any evidence to suggest otherwise, we are assuming that the perceptions offered by our participants reflect real issues in the community, but acknowledge that perceptions are not always correct. That said, and assuming that the perceived issues are, in fact, real, we offer the following changes for leadership to consider.

- *Consider formally managing the cyberofficer 17D and 17S positions as distinct career fields.* A broad array of negative comments heard during our discussions were fundamentally related to the tension between the functionally different jobs that exist within the 17D community. These tensions affect recruiting, training, career development, and ultimately retention (a consequence of low job satisfaction). One possible way to alleviate some of the tension is to formally manage 17D and 17S operators as distinct career fields, analogous to the different pilot career fields (fighter, mobility, and others). Separating the career fields would not preclude common core training or significant flow of personnel across career fields as functional roles evolve over time. The 17D career field is in transition, however, and there may be value in exposing cyber operators to the full range of missions within a single career field—so a decision to separate the career field could be premature. Ultimately, policymakers should weigh the costs and benefits of this course of action.

- *Create opportunities for cyber officers to pursue technical depth.* A related and cross-cutting theme that emerged in both the research literature and interviews is the strong desire of personnel working in cyber to pursue and maintain technical depth. Air Force cyber operators are concerned about being pulled away from technical duties and relegated to administrative duties or leadership positions. Many of our participants believe that technical depth is uniquely important in the cyber workforce, and operational proficiency should be a priority amid other career development goals. One model might be for career field management to allow for the development of depth in the same way that it is allowed among aircrew personnel. Regardless, this recommendation assumes that technical depth is both desired by some personnel (likely a fair assumption, given our findings) and that technical depth would be beneficial for cyber mission success in the Air Force. The first alone may be sufficient to justify establishing a technical track for purposes of increasing retention. The second, however, may be worth exploring further through additional research.

- *Continue to prioritize technical backgrounds in accessions, with pathways for candidates to demonstrate potential in other ways.* Prior research suggests that technical backgrounds should be preferred, but organizations should also look for cyber talent in populations comprising people who do not hold computer science or engineering degrees. Thus, the best strategy currently is to pursue candidates with technical backgrounds while also supporting opportunities for candidates to demonstrate cyber potential in other ways, such as cyber competitions. Policymakers should evaluate whether additional recruiting resources are necessary to bring in candidates with the right skill mix. That said, this too assumes that perceptions about certain educational backgrounds being beneficial for cyber officer effectiveness are correct. This could also be further explored through additional research.

- *Closely monitor retention and be prepared to use the full spectrum of retention tools.* Civilian demand for cyber expertise is strong. The research literature and interview participants both point to retention drivers in the areas of compensation, quality of life, and training and career development opportunities—all of which translate into job satisfaction. There is also evidence that retention can be manageable despite strong civilian demand. Lastly, our examination of retention among experienced 17S officers suggests that these personnel are leaving at a higher rate than that of the rest of the career field. Thus it would be wise to closely monitor 17D subgroup retention patterns and address the drivers of low retention as much as possible. Within the 17D community, those with 17S experience can be identified, but more detailed subgroup information (e.g., whether that assignment involves offensive versus defensive operations) is not currently recorded in the Air Force's personnel data files.
- *Track and evaluate other outcomes of interest.* Valuable insights could be gained from the measurement and tracking of a range of additional variables, including the performance and effectiveness of cyber operators; applicant and selectee characteristics; perceptions about the job at various points in the career lifespan (including at the applicant stage); and exit interview information from personnel who are leaving. Such information could be used in a variety of ways, including to further confirm which KSAOs are most central to success; to explore how well the Air Force is recruiting or retaining people with the right KSAOs; to better manage expectations of new personnel, address concerns of those leaving, and market the career field to new high potential candidates; and to evaluate the success of any retention or recruiting initiatives. Unless the Air Force begins collecting and intentionally tracking this information now and continues to do so going forward, the opportunities for exploration will be limited only to the information on hand, which at this point is only a limited amount of information.
- *Ensure sufficient agility in training, tactics, and acquisition.* As noted above, a salient theme in discussions with SMEs was the perception that the Air Force is not postured to keep pace with the rapidly evolving nature of the cyber domain. At minimum, training content needs to be updated constantly and adapted to student backgrounds, and continuation training needs to be robust and constantly evolving. Maintaining state-of-the-art skills is important to cybersecurity professionals. As such, developing and sustaining agile training opportunities could have a measurable effect on the retention and effectiveness of cyber operators. In addition, our participants expressed concerns about lack of agility in acquisitions and in a lack of authority to make the decisions needed to address local commander needs. These too may be leading to frustration, and ultimately may factor into decisions by some to leave. However, this issue of a lack of agility is another example of a perception about the work environment that may or may not prove to be based in fact. Further research measuring how agile training, tactics, and acquisition actually are in the cyber community may therefore be warranted. If no problems with agility are uncovered, then efforts should be made to further explore the root of this misperception.
- *Teach such concepts as warfighting, the mission, strategic thinking, and operational planning at all levels.* Interview participants repeatedly pointed to warfighting and understanding the mission set as areas of expertise that define a high-quality 17D but are woefully underdeveloped within the force. They believed strongly that people needed a much richer understanding of these topics in general and that the Air Force needs to

begin instilling them at much earlier points in one's career (starting as early as undergraduate cyberspace training).

- *Establish and communicate a strategic vision for the career field and link it to the tactical-level work.* There appears to be a large disconnect between the work taking place at the tactical level and the strategic cyber mission that leadership is articulating. Feedback on how maintenance and support activities are helping the fight is important to cyber personnel. The disconnect affects morale and efficiency of operations. Many of our participants suggested that responsibility for establishing this link is on midlevel leaders. But they also believe that the diffusion of responsibility at the highest levels of cyber leadership makes it difficult to articulate a singular vision in a way that will successfully permeate the enterprise at all levels.

- *Establish a forum through which to collect innovative ideas for managing the cyber career field.* Officers in the 17D career field may have a number of innovative ideas for how to improve the services the cyber workforce provides and for managing the career field in a way that could improve recruiting and retention. In a few instances, our participants brainstormed, coming up with some interesting ideas for new ways of doing business that could potentially help address various concerns within the workforce. Currently there is no system in place for personnel to brainstorm regarding how to revolutionize the way cyber does business. Establishing such a forum could be an effective way of gathering innovative ideas to improve both the services the cyber workforce provides to the Air Force and job satisfaction among cyber personnel.

- *Establish enterprise-wide and forward-thinking approaches.* The existence of outdated legacy systems (e.g., IT, communications, hardware, and weapon systems) and the fact that some organizations refuse to update or adopt common technology are inefficiencies that cause increased workload and general frustration within the cyber community. In order for the Air Force to be a formidable cyber force against its adversaries, officers believe that it is critical to place a high priority on investments in cutting-edge technology, training, and approaches to doing business. Doing so, however, would require the Air Force to foster an environment that embraces new technologies and cutting-edge concepts. Yet, according to our participants' perspectives, when it comes to supporting new technologies and new ideas in the cyber domain, the Air Force is lagging.

- *Explore recruiting and retention challenges in the Air Force enlisted and civilian cyber communities.* The civilian cyber community faces similar challenges in finding and attracting qualified personnel, and according to some of our participants, is experiencing extremely high levels of turnover in some cases. Retaining enlisted personnel, particularly the highest skilled personnel, could become increasingly difficult in the face of the pay differential with the civilian marketplace. Replicating this type of study with civilian and enlisted personnel could help to identify the most effective approaches to managing cyber talent in these communities.

Additional Caveats to Our Recommendations

The goal of this study was to explore attitudes relating to and perceptions about major drivers of retention in the cyber officer workforce. This study was designed to be exploratory, meaning that we held open-ended discussions where we asked participants to tell us their own top concerns. This has two main benefits. First, it does not presume that we know in advance what those concerns will be; as such, participants are not primed by the researchers to focus on a particular topic. Second, it allows us the opportunity to fully explore what participants mean when they express a concern by asking for examples, probing for more information, and asking follow-on questions.

However, there are also limitations to the approach. For example, one limitation to this type of study design is that it does not typically have as large of a sample as might occur on a larger-scale survey because of time and resource constraints. This limits the power of the study to detect significant differences between groups. Another potential downside is that participation may not necessarily be representative of all members of the community since not all locations can be visited in person (a survey can more easily sample participants from all locations, although not all surveys do). Although those are potential limitations of this type of design, we took steps to combat those limitations by holding discussions at a range of diverse bases and with a large number of participants.

An additional concern commonly raised about participation in focus groups such as these is that the people who volunteer to participate may be particularly dissatisfied and therefore not representative of the career field as a whole. Two points regarding this are worth making. First, we asked participants to tell us what they like about their job, in part to determine whether they are truly disgruntled. If they are, we would expect that they would have a hard time coming up with positive things to say. In fact, we did hear numerous positives from our participants, with some describing plenty of reasons why they would like to stay in addition to offering thoughtful insights into reasons why they or others might be driven to leave. In addition, the survey results show that many of our participants are satisfied with their career. Second, even if we did end up with people who were more dissatisfied than the others within the career field, it may not be problematic for the goal of this particular study. That is, if the goal is to identify ideas for how to keep more personnel, talking only with the people who are dissatisfied might still provide a number of useful insights.

As noted previously, it is important to point out that this study was designed to describe the workforce's perceptions and views regarding the drivers of retention and recruiting within the cyber community. These views and perceptions are an excellent initial source for recommending initiatives that could improve retention and recruiting; however, we cannot know from those perceptions alone whether those initiatives will be successful and, if so, how successful. It is also not known whether any of the perceptions identified here represent misperceptions, and that these misperceptions themselves are all that need to be addressed. As a result, additional research should be undertaken to explore any areas where leadership believes the prevailing perception is simply a misperception. In addition, for those areas where the perception is believed to be based in fact, research should be undertaken to measure the impacts on recruiting, retention, and satisfaction within the community that result from the Air Force adopting any of the recommendations we offer above. The results of that research should inform further changes to any initiatives to address retention and recruiting going forward.

Looking Ahead

To lead in cyber, the Air Force needs to be proactive, not reactive. Competition with the private sector for top talent will only increase as demands for cyberspace professionals rise nationally. Thus, it is not prudent for the Air Force to wait for a problem to arise or to worsen before acting. Cyber is a fast-moving field, and its evolving nature affects the interests of the professionals working within it.

The insights gained through this study point to areas where initial steps can be taken to increase job satisfaction, improve retention, and reshape how the Air Force markets its cyber job opportunities to the public. Improving training content and opportunities throughout the careers of cyber personnel is an example of the type of action that could have significant payoff, given the importance that cyberspace professionals place on staying current in their field. Ensuring that cyber personnel can remain focused on operational duties for longer in their careers without fear of being transferred to administrative or leadership positions (where technical skill atrophy is likely to occur) is another example. And both of these actions have precedent in other career fields. But being responsive to the workforce is a continuous process. It will mean taking the pulse of the workforce at regular intervals to make sure that the steps taken are having the desired results and the Air Force is able to recruit and retain the high-quality talent essential for mission success.

Acknowledgments

Many people assisted us in this project, and we appreciate the time and effort they contributed. We thank our project sponsor, Maj Gen Patrick C. Higby (SAF/CIO A6S), as well as our project points of contact, Lt Col Joseph Wingo (SAF/CIO A6SF), Capt Michelle "Boom" Bostic (SAF/CIO A6SF), and 2nd Lt Gloria Williams (SAF/CIO A6SF), who provided helpful guidance through the project and assisted us in identifying SMEs, cyber workforce locations for us to recruit from for our interviews, and initial contacts at each base.

We conducted interviews with members of the cyber workforce at seven air bases. At each site, individuals assisted us in numerous ways, from making initial points of contact, to recruiting and contacting focus group participants, to serving as focus group site coordinators. The airmen named here were instrumental in the success of our work; they were generous with their time, and we are grateful for each of their contributions:

- Hickam Air Force Base: Capt Robert Dawson, focus group site coordinator; Col Glen M. Genove; and Maj Kurt Weissgerber
- Scott Air Force Base: 1st Lt Alex D. Nelson, focus group site coordinator; Lt Col Robert Biggers; and Col Roger R. Vrooman
- Fort Meade: 2nd Lt Mohammad U. Ashraf, focus group site coordinator; Lt Col Rebecca Lange; and Maj Christopher Quinlan
- Peterson Air Force Base: 1st Lt George Peterson, focus group site coordinator; Col Charles F. Arnold; and Lt Col Heather Uhl
- Hurlburt Field and Eglin Air Force Base: Maj Stephanie Baskett, Capt Steven Blose, Maj Gilberto Perez, Thomas Person, and Lt Col Angela Waters, who served as focus group site coordinators; Col Chad Lemaire; and Col William C. Waynick II
- Lackland Air Force Base: TSgt Deandra Flowers, SSgt Calissa Fulton, Capt Sean Guerrero, Lt Col Jonathan Joshua, and Capt Oscar Nunez, focus group site coordinators; SMSgt Ameerah Beyahbrewer; Maj Steven Chetelat; Lt Col Robert Giovannetti; Col Michelle Hayworth, Col Bradley Pyburn, Col Gregory Schechtman; and Lt Col Andrew Vanderziel
- Robbins Air Force Base: Capt Jonathan W. Hampe.

We also thank each of our SMEs, mentioned by name in the body of this report, as well as our many anonymous 17D interview participants, for their willing participation and for enriching our research with their insights.

At the RAND Corporation we thank several people who were instrumental in seeing this project to completion: Barbara Bicksler, for her assistance in editing and revising the final report; Julie Ann Tajiri, for her assistance in preparing our travel arrangements to various base locations; Ryan Haberman, Etienne Rosas, and Ben Smith, for their hard work coding our focus group transcripts and our many transcribers who worked tirelessly to the very end (e.g., Sohaela Amiri, Samantha DiNicola, Ryan Haberman, Emily Haskel, Luke Irwin, Cedric Kenney, Claudia Rodriguez, Nima Shahidinia, and Ben Smith). Finally, we thank our reviewers for their thoughtful comments, which lead to significant improvements to this report.

Abbreviations

24 AF	24th Air Force
ACC	Air Combat Command
AF/A1	Deputy Chief of Staff for Manpower, Personnel and Services, Headquarters U.S. Air Force
AFDD	Air Force Doctrine Document
AFIT	Air Force Institute of Technology
AFNet	Air Force Network
AFOCD	*Air Force Officer Classification Directory*
AFSC	Air Force Specialty Code
AFSPC	Air Force Space Command
AOC	Air Operations Center
CGO	company grade officer
CMF	Cyber Mission Force
COA	course of action
CWO	chief warrant officer
CWS	*Cyberspace Workforce Strategy*
CYOS	commissioned year of service
DCO	defensive cyber operations
DoD	Department of Defense
DoDIN	Department of Defense Information Network
DT	development team
FEVS	Federal Employee Viewpoint Survey
FGO	field grade officer
GAO	Government Accountability Office
IQT	Initial Qualification Training
IST	Initial Skills Training
IT	information technology

JP	Joint Publication
KSAOs	knowledge, skills, abilities, and other characteristics
MQT	Mission Qualification Training
OCO	offensive cyber operations
PAF	RAND Project AIR FORCE
POC	points of contact
ROTC	Reserve Officers' Training Corps
SME	subject matter expert
STEM	science, technology, engineering, and mathematics
UCT	Undergraduate Cyber Training
UPT	Undergraduate Pilot Training
USCYBERCOM	U.S. Cyber Command

1. Introduction

Cybersecurity is one of the most serious economic and national security challenges we face as a nation. Given the U.S. Air Force mission to "fly, fight and win in air, space and cyberspace," addressing this potential security threat falls squarely within the Air Force's responsibility. However, many are concerned about the current health and future state of the Air Force's cyberspace community. Sen John McCain voiced his concerns in an opening statement during a May 9, 2017, hearing on the posture of U.S. Cyber Command:

> As for the efforts at the Department of Defense, I understand that Cyber Command is still on track to reaching full operational capability for the training of the Cyber Mission Force in the fall of 2018. But unless we see dramatic changes in future budgets, I am concerned these forces will lack the tools required to protect, deter, and respond to malicious cyber behavior. In short, unless the services begin to prioritize and deliver the cyber weapons systems necessary to fight in cyberspace, we are heading down the path to a hollow cyber force. (U.S. Senate Committee on Armed Services, 2017)

Consistent with this statement, the Air Force has acknowledged that it is facing a large shortage of cyber field grade officers (FGOs, O-4 to O-6) in the near and long term, raising concerns about retention now and in the future. The fact that demand for skilled cyber officers in both the Air Force and joint environments is high only exacerbates that concern.[1] In addition, the Air Force faces stiff competition with the private sector in attracting and retaining top cyber talent; this could make it difficult to build and maintain a highly capable cyber workforce. Finally, because some airmen in the cyber field receive extensive highly technical training that further increases their marketability, the Air Force is concerned that it may lose talented personnel to competition with the private sector.

Put simply, there is concern among Air Force officials that retention in the officer cyber community may become challenging. Because of these concerns, Air Force leadership asked RAND Project AIR FORCE (PAF) to explore perspectives within the Air Force cyber operations officer (17D) workforce on the major drivers of attraction to and retention in the career field and to recommend ideas for initiatives to help identify, recruit, and retain successful cyber personnel.

Our sponsor's goals for the study were broad. Maj Gen Patrick C. Higby (SAF/CIO A6S), director of cyberspace strategy and policy for the Office of Information Dominance and chief information officer for the Office of the Secretary of the Air Force, was particularly interested in understanding the entire landscape of concerns within the workforce, especially because his

---

[1] We use *cyber officer* and *cyberspace operations officer* interchangeably throughout this report.

office's current sense of the prevailing concerns was based largely on anecdotes offered by leadership within the force and informal input gained though social media and other places where personnel are known to voice concerns. Both are relevant places to start, but neither is rigorous enough to stand up to heavy scrutiny. He therefore was interested in having PAF conduct a more systematic effort exploring the entirety of their concerns. That information could then serve as a starting point for identifying potential recruiting and retention initiatives for the workforce.

In addition, in discussing the project with the sponsor it became clear that the Air Force was also particularly concerned with attracting and retaining the *right* officers (i.e., those that would be the best cyber officers). As a result, we saw a need for additional exploration of which cyber officer qualities were viewed as especially important for ensuring cyber mission success.

Lastly, the sponsor's office was preparing to conduct a large-scale survey of cyber officer perceptions at some point in the future. The PAF study presented an opportunity to establish a small baseline set of responses to a wide range of attitudinal items that could be used for comparison to that or other future survey efforts within the cyber workforce. It also afforded an opportunity to benchmark the cyber workforce's views collected in this study against responses by the broader Air Force collected in other surveys.

Based on this information, we set the following overarching goals for the study:

1. Summarize current views on what defines a high-quality cyber officer
2. Identify the perceived drivers of attraction to and retention in the career field
3. Identify other perceived sources of dissatisfaction
4. Provide a small set of responses to attitudinal survey items to serve as an initial look and baseline for future efforts
5. Use these results as a starting point for outlining a set of potential suggested changes to impact retention and recruiting of cyber officers down the road.

Additional details on our approach can be found later in this chapter and in Chapter Two.

A Brief Overview of the 17D Cyber Officer Career Field

The Air Force's 17D cyber officer workforce is responsible for three main types of activities: offensive cyber operations (OCO) (launching cyberattacks against our adversaries); defensive cyber operations (DCO, which defend Air Force and Department of Defense networks against attacks by an adversary); and Department of Defense Information Network (DoDIN) operations (development, support and maintenance of various DoDIN systems).

The type of activity in which someone is engaged depends on the duty assignment he or she holds. The first two types of activities (OCO and DCO) are associated with the 17S Air Force Specialty Code (AFSC) duty designator, and only a subset of cyber officers serve in those types of assignments. Within 17S assignments, the duties are typically either focused on OCO, or DCO, but not usually both. DoDIN operations jobs—designated as 17D duty assignments—

represent the remainder of the career field's duty assignments. These include operations and mission assurance for Air Force weapon systems and platforms, as well as providing information technology (IT) support for personnel at the base level.

The 17D cyber operations officer career field was established in 2010. Prior to 2010, 17D-type work was performed by personnel under a different career field designator: 33S communications and information officers. In 2010, members of the 33S community transitioned to the new AFSC designator and the 33S career field was eliminated. Around 2015, several years after the new 17D career field was established, the Air Force established the 17S designator for offensive/defensive cyber duty assignments. Note that 17D is both a duty assignment designator and a career field designator, whereas 17S is only an assignment designator. That is, some members of the 17D career field are in 17S duty assignments, and some are in 17D assignments.

For the complete 2017 *Air Force Officer Classification Directory* (AFOCD) entry describing the 17D and 17S specialty codes, see Appendix A.

Explaining the Shortage of Field Grade Officers

As noted above, the 17D career field has a shortage of officers in the field grade ranks to fill its funded requirements. This issue is illustrated in Figure 1.1, which provides a number of useful insights into some of the issues contributing to the perception that retention and recruiting of officers is a problem. The figure illustrates three key pieces of information about the cyber officer workforce: number of funded requirements, an example sustainment profile, and the number of 17D officers as of March 2017.

In the case of requirements, in 2017 there were 2,514 funded positions allocated to cyber officers. In Figure 1.1, those requirements (shown as the gray line) are spread across commissioned years of service (CYOS) ranging from 0 to 30, taking into consideration on the grade requirements specified for that position. That is, certain positions within the cyber community require that they be filled by an FGO, because they require experience commensurate with that level of CYOS. The position requirements in the figure are distributed across the CYOS that are appropriate to the grade requirements for the position. The sustainment line (in red) reflects the number of officers in the career field based on retention rates and sustained accessions (of 260 airmen per year). The sustainment profile contains 3,184 positions, which includes an extra 670 requirements for student, transient, and personnel holdees, as well as institutional requirements; airmen in these statuses are unavailable to fill funded requirements. Blue bars in the figure illustrate numbers of personnel in the career field at each CYOS.

As noted above, each of these pieces of information can provide insights into why retention is considered a concern. For example, the blue bars show the detrimental impact of past force-reduction efforts—commonly referred to as a "bathtub effect"—where the number of personnel at certain grades is low relative to the grade groups above and below them. Because there is very little opportunity to increase personnel numbers through lateral entry into the career field (that is, personnel typically are only permitted to enter the career field at the low ranks), the bathtub remains, following the affected cohorts as they progress through their career. An example of this effect is illustrated by the blue bars in Figure 1.1, where a bathtub can be seen in CYOS 5, 6, 8, 9, and 10. This bathtub means that there is an imbalance in the experience levels of personnel, with fewer personnel in the middle CYOS years than there ought to be relative to the numbers of personnel in the higher and lower CYOS years. This bathtub is part of what explains the FGO-level officer shortage.

In addition, Figure 1.1 shows that the number of funded requirements is not in line with the grade levels that would be available under the sustainment profile, even without the bathtub effect to contend with. That is, years where funded requirements (shown in green) are higher than the sustainment line (shown in red) are years in which shortages will likely always exist and funded authorizations are unsustainable. In the figure, shortages begin in CYOS 10, at the O-4 rank, and continue at a declining level through CYOS 19. This means that the Air Force cannot develop enough officers in the career field to meet the O-4 requirements with the current planned retention pattern shown by the sustainment profile. In other words, the FGO shortfall is not just an immediate concern; it is a symptom of a larger issue—namely, that the number of requirements for FGOs is out of balance with number of requirements for company grade officers (CGOs, O-1 to O-3), making the career field by definition unsustainable.

Figure 1.1. Cyber Sustainment Profile and Inventory

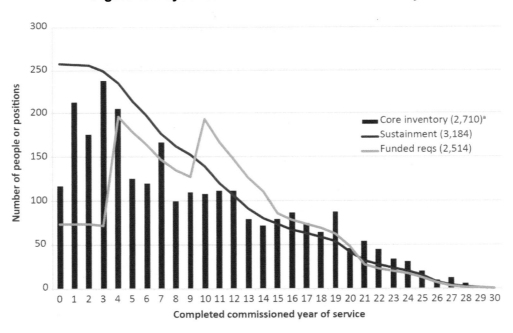

SOURCE: This figure was originally designed by Jerry Diaz (AF/A1 PF). We replicated the figure using Air Force Personnel Center personnel and manning data files, sustainment based on five-year retention for 2011–2015, and requirements from the end of FY 2016.
[a] Core inventory figures are valid as of March 31, 2017.

More specifically, in the sustainment profile, only 36 percent of officers are expected to be in field grade ranks, but the actual funded requirements call for 51 percent of officers at field grades. As a result, there will still be a dire FGO shortage, even when overall total numbers of personnel in the career field appear healthy.

This imbalance in the numbers of FGOs needed relative to CGOs has not always existed. Figure 1.2 shows how the percentage of field grade officer requirements has changed over time. The green line is the entire 17D career field, while the red and blue lines split that requirement into joint positions (between the Office of the Secretary of Defense and combatant commands) and positions internal to the Air Force, respectively. Joint locations require nearly 80 percent of their positions to be filled by field grade officers, but even service requirements alone have exceeded the 36 percent field grade ratio in the sustainment profile during the past decade.

Figure 1.2. Percentages of Cyber Jobs that Require Field Grade Officers, by Fiscal Year

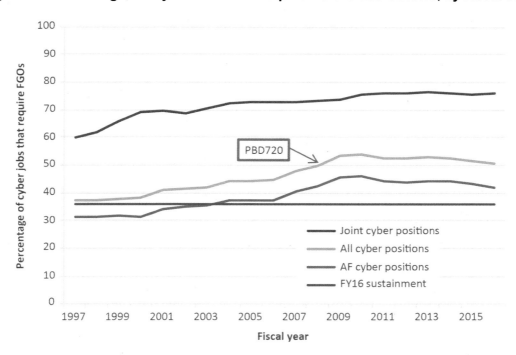

Part of the imbalance stems from career field cuts that occurred between 2007 and 2009, due to Program Budget Decision 720, which the Air Force implemented mostly through company grade reductions, driving the field grade ratio higher.[2] But even before that period, the career field requirements for field grade officers were already unsustainable due in large part to a steady diet of reductions from the late 1990s that favored cuts to company grade over field grade positions.

---

[2] Program Budget Decision 720 was a 2007 budget initiative to cut 40,000 active duty and total force members and retire older aircraft for system recapitalization and modernization.

Recognizing that the FGO requirements imbalance is part of the problem, it is worth noting that improving the balance of FGO to CGO requirements would be an important step in addressing the officer retention problem, and one that ultimately needs to be addressed to ensure sustainable long-term career field health. This issue is being addressed by SAF/CIO through a thorough review of the FGO requirements to determine which, if any, could be shifted to a CGO billet. However, it is unlikely that many of the FGO positions will change, as there is an insatiable demand for experienced 17D personnel, and it is experience that can only be gained through years of training in the classroom and on the job. Given that demand for FGO experience is not likely to wane, leadership is not hopeful that simple conversion of FGO billets to other types of positions will solve the problem, at least not in its entirety.[3]

Going on that assumption, and recognizing that the existing bathtub effect is not likely to resolve itself for years to come, the career field likely will still need to find ways to fill as many FGO positions as it can. However, to do that, it simply must retain more personnel than would be typical for most career fields in the Air Force.[4] It needs to aim for a higher sustainment profile. And to accomplish that, it needs a solid understanding of why people may want to leave the career field in order to retain as many airmen as it can.

Exploring Retention Rates Within the Cyber Community

Several people we spoke with over the course of this study have stated that retention within the 17D community is considered good relative to that of other career fields. In support of that belief, they cite that the overall retention profile observed for 17Ds aligns well with the profile identified in Figure 1.1. Nonetheless, given that the FGO/CGO imbalance in requirements explained in the previous section has not yet been resolved, and the bathtub from CYOS 5 to CYOS 10 cannot easily be filled, retention is still a concern even if it matches the levels seen in other career fields. As a result, leadership has been interested in finding ways to keep even more personnel, above and beyond that typically retained in other career fields.

However, before seeking out drivers of even better retention, we sought to confirm that retention is in fact good relative to other career fields and explore the retention profile for 17Ds a bit further, going beyond just looking at 17Ds as a whole. More specifically, one concern

---

[3] That said, the importance of addressing the career field planning problem should not be ignored. The FGO requirements imbalance needs to be fixed for the sustainability of the career field in the long term. If the FGO requirements are not balanced with the CGO requirements, the career field will appear undermanned at the FGO levels in perpetuity, forever impacting the career field's ability to successfully execute the mission expected of it. Other ways to address this include increasing the number of accessions to raise the sustainability line to a point where it meets the level of FGO positions, or allowing lateral entry of more experienced personnel into the career field from other Air Force occupations, directly from industry, or both.

[4] Note that another way to help address this issue is to ensure faster promotion of cyber personnel to O-4, which may be an additional stopgap option (Secretary of the Air Force Public Affairs, 2017).

discussed by members of the cyber officer community is that those involved in 17S jobs may be dismayed by the inability to stay technical or stay in a 17S position, and are therefore more likely to want to leave.[5] To explore this we examined retention differences between those who have held a 17S job in the last two years and those who have not, using two years of retention data. Figure 1.3 shows the results of that examination by displaying cumulative retention rates (i.e., proportions of personnel who are still on active duty a year later) separately for the two groups of cyber personnel. Figure 1.3 also includes a retention line for all nonrated line officers over the same two-year period, for comparison.[6]

Figure 1.3. Retention Rates by Type of Assignment Held in the Last Two Years (17D Versus 17S)

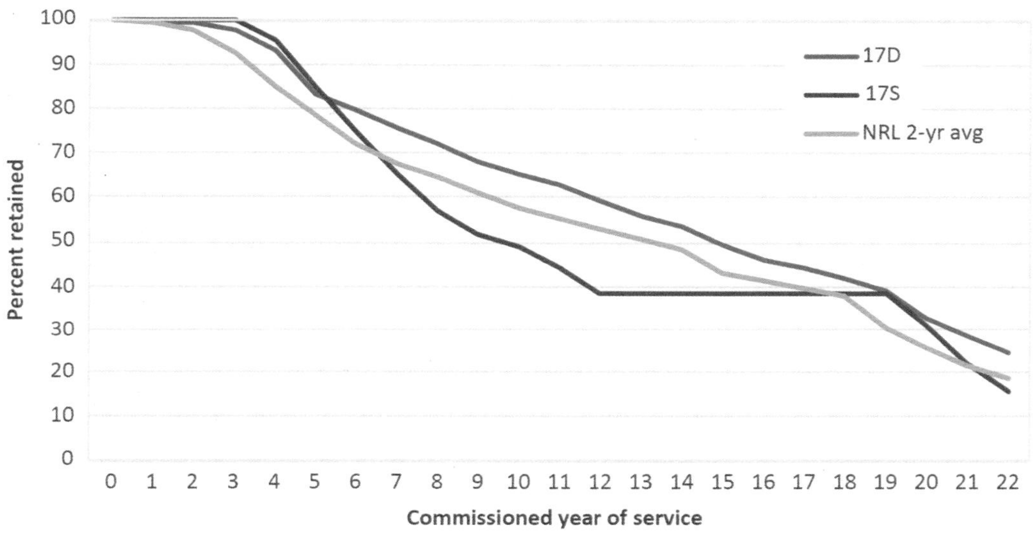

NOTE: NRL = nonrated line officers; 17S, *n* = 827; 17D, *n* = 3,882; NRL, *n* = 48,937.

Caveats Regarding Our 17D Retention Estimates

Before discussing the implications of Figure 1.3, some important limitations about the data are worth noting. One major limitation is that we are only able to include people holding a 17S job in the last two years because (as noted above) the 17S jobs have only been on the books since 2015. Prior to that, 17S did not exist as an assignment designator. This necessarily constrains the amount of data that we can display, which in turn limits the interpretation of the figure in several important ways.

---

[5] Currently, all cyber officers are members of the 17D AFSC, but are conceptually separated based on assignment into 17D (DoDIN) or 17S (DCO and OCO). See Appendix A for background on the 17D career field and discussion of the cyber mission within the Air Force.

[6] The nonrated line officer retention data includes data from the 17D workforce.

First, for purposes of career field planning, at least five years of retention data is preferred for establishing stable retention profiles. Given that we only have two years in these data, we strongly advise updating this information over the next few years to see if there is still a notable difference between the 17S and 17D lines. The results shown here should therefore be considered preliminary until additional data can be collected.

Second, because we only have two years of data and 17S assignments represent a small fraction of the billets, it means that sample sizes for the 17S retention line are small relative to that of the 17D retention line (827 versus 3,882). However, in the important years (between 6 and 10 CYOS) where we see the relatively lower retention rates, 17S sample sizes range from 40 to 70, which are large enough to provide fairly stable estimates of retention at those points.[7]

Third, it is important to note that offensive and defensive positions existed before the 17S designator was established. This means that some of the people classified as 17D-only in our figure, may have held an offensive or defensive assignment more than 2 years ago. Given this, the 17S data in the figure need to be carefully interpreted as showing us only the rates of people retaining who have held a 17S assignment *recently* in their career. Likewise, the 17D line shows us rates of people retaining who have *not recently* held a 17S assignment in their career.

It is also important to note that cyber work itself has changed substantively over the years, (separate from the changes to the AFSC designator) because technology itself has changed. As a result, the requirements for a 17D today are necessarily different from what was expected of 33Ss ten or fifteen years ago, when communications technology was simpler. Now the job is much more technical, requiring greater skill and expertise. As a result, the characteristics of the people in the career field have changed, with more emphasis on science, technology, engineering, and mathematics (STEM) and technical backgrounds in the career field today than there had been in the 33S career field of the past. As such, the retention line patterns shown in Figure 1.3 (where the upper CYOS years are based on people who spent much of their career as 33Ss) may not be indicative of retention in the future in this 17D career field. This too suggests that close looks at retention within the 17D workforce going forward are likely warranted for several years to come.

Lastly, we note that the figure cannot tell us anything about causality. For example, it does not tell us whether holding a 17S assignment causes people to leave at a higher rate, or whether people who tend to get assigned to a 17S duty already have a higher proclivity to leave and would do so at higher rates regardless of which type of duty assignment they were ultimately given. As noted below, there are likely some important aptitude differences (and potentially

---

[7] As a rule of thumb, sample sizes of 25 or 30 are generally accepted as a desired minimum to provide stable estimates of population percentages. Between CYOS 2 and 13, the sample sizes for any single proportion estimate range from 29 to 94 for the 17S line and 105 to 306 for the 17D line. In those CYOS years the sample sizes are large enough that the differences between the lines are statistically significant at the point where the lines noticeably diverge. The lowest sample size in the figure is for the 17S line at CYOS 22 years, where $n = 7$.

8

other demographic differences) between the two groups which may partly account for the differences.

Implications of Our 17D Retention Estimates

For all the reasons outlined above, Figure 1.3 should be viewed only as an initial exploration of this issue, not a definitive answer regarding retention of personnel holding 17D vs. 17S assignments. Nevertheless, as an initial exploration, the figure does reveal two interesting findings worth noting.

First, it shows that people with only 17D assignments in the last few years retain about as well as other AFSCs in the Air Force. That is, the 17D-only retention line is about parallel to that of the nonrated line officers regardless of CYOS year. This suggests that at the typical points when officers can leave (such as at the end of their active duty service commitment), the proportion of 17Ds leaving from that retention line is not any higher than that in other career fields.

Second, it is also clear from Figure 1.3 that anyone who has held a 17S job in the last few years is leaving service at a higher rate, specifically between six and ten years of commissioned service.[8] This finding, although still preliminary, raises serious concerns that the Air Force's offensive and defensive capability (i.e., personnel with 17S experience) may be disproportionately affected by retention problems.[9] Furthermore, given that 17S assignments have historically been allocated to the highest-performing individuals within the 17D community, including those ranked at the top of their class in Undergraduate Cyber Training (UCT), this suggests that some of the most talented and technically competent members of the community are being lost at high rates.

Recognizing that these losses ultimately could affect the Air Force's ability to achieve its cyber warfighting mission, it is particularly important to explore in detail concerns by members of the cyber workforce community to get a sense for what might be driving retention. That was the primary goal of the research effort described in this report, and our approach to doing so is described below.

Approach and Organization of This Report

To help the Air Force gain insights into key drivers for attracting and retaining personnel into the 17D career field and key characteristics of high-performing cyber personnel, we pursued several lines of research.

---

[8] After personnel got to 12 years of service, we saw no separations until the 20-year mark. Note, however, that the potential impact of the recently enacted "blended" retirement system on retention rates up to the 20-year point cannot yet be assessed, but it may change how retention looks in the future.

[9] This is of concern regardless of whether holding 17S assignments is partly a cause of the retention problem or whether it is entirely a result of demographic differences (such as aptitude) that may exist between the two groups.

First, we reviewed what is already known about the issues within the 17D community and about knowledge, skills, abilities, and other characteristics (KSAOs) needed in the cyber workforce. We started by gathering background information about the issues facing the career field by talking with a range of cyber officer subject matter experts (SMEs). We supplemented that by reviewing existing articles published about the issues within the community and research on the cyber workforce in the Air Force and the private sector. Background on those issues and existing research on the community are summarized in Appendixes B and C. Existing research on the KSAOs needed in the cyber workforce is discussed in Chapter Three.

Second, we explored Air Force personnel data files to better understand key characteristics of the Air Force's cyber workforce. The results of our exploration of retention rates by type of assignment (17D versus 17S) were discussed earlier in this chapter.

Third, we conducted a series of interviews with three key populations to identify potential drivers of retention and recruiting and to define key KSAOs needed in the 17D workforce. The first interview population was a *series of SMEs within the 17D community.* These included people who hold key leadership or oversight positions within the community—for example, wing commander, career field manager, cyber assignment decisions, 24th Air Force (24 AF) commander, members of the development teams (DTs), and others. The second population was *members of the 17D workforce* at the lieutenant colonel level and below. We conducted group and individual interviews at several air bases, holding discussions separately by work type and by FGO and CGO rank status. Along with focus group discussions, we administered a questionnaire to participants that asked about their satisfaction with various aspects of the career field and their views on KSAOs needed within the community.

Lastly, we spoke with a handful of private-sector cyber specialists to get their insights into the Air Force's recruiting and retention challenges. Early informal discussions with cyber officer SMEs and our review of existing literature helped to inform the questions we asked of our three interview populations.

The methodology used in conducting the interviews is discussed in detail in Chapter Two. Chapter Three contains our findings on desirable KSAOs for the cyber workforce as described during interviews with the 17D workforce, as well as the literature review. Chapter Four focuses on sources of dissatisfaction and possible drivers of retention and recruiting identified through discussions with the 17D workforce. Comments from the SMEs and private-sector specialists echoed many of the 17D workforce comments and are therefore duplicative of the information discussed in Chapter Four. Chapter Five provides a synthesis of the entirety of the work and its implications for possible initiatives to improve the attraction and retention of high-quality 17Ds going forward. Conclusions and recommendations are also contained in Chapter Five.

2. Our Approach to the Interviews

Our methodology centered on interviews conducted with members of the 17D career field at all levels—members of the 17D workforce and more senior Air Force SMEs. In addition, we also held conversations with a few individuals in the cybersecurity and IT private sector. This chapter describes the approach we used in conducting these interviews and the number and characteristics of participants in each of the three broad groups.

Interviews with the 17D Workforce

Participants from the 17D workforce were invited to participate in in-person or phone interviews.[1] We also asked participants to complete paper-and-pencil surveys prior to the discussion.

Discussions with Participants

Our research team held a total of 68 discussions with members of the 17D workforce (50 in person, and 18 by phone). Participants were recruited from Joint Base Pearl Harbor–Hickam; Scott Air Force Base; Fort Meade; Peterson and Schriever Air Force Bases (discussions were held at Peterson), Joint Base San Antonio–Lackland (discussions were held at Lackland), Hurlburt Field and Eglin Air Force Base (discussion were held at Hurlburt); and Robins Air Force Base (discussions were held remotely by phone). The majority of our participants were stationed at these locations at the time of our interviews, but a few individuals volunteered to participate who were on temporary duty assignment or who heard about the focus groups but were stationed at other bases in the United States or around the world. Table 2.1 shows the number of participants from each location with seven or more participants. To protect confidentiality, participants from the remaining locations (Robins, Hickam, and elsewhere) were grouped together for purposes of reporting sample sizes.

---

[1] Participants were recruited through announcements made by point of contacts (POCs) identified at each base. Those POCs were named by cyber leadership at the base (typically a colonel in some sort of command position) and tasked with getting the word out and coordinating private rooms for our discussions. Recruiting was conducted through in-person oral announcements made to cyber work groups, word of mouth, and emails sent to base-level cyber workforce aliases.

Table 2.1. Number and Location of Cyber Workforce Interview Participants

Location	Number of Participants
Joint Base San Antonio–Lackland	19
Fort Meade	14
Peterson and Schriever Air Force Bases	8
Hurlburt Field and Eglin Air Force Base	8
Scott Air Force Base	7
Other Base Locations	12

Some of the in-person discussions were held as group interviews, with two or more participants at a time (ranging from two to seven per group); however, in many cases only one person was available at a given time and the discussion was therefore held as an individual interview. Phone discussions were held one participant at a time. The largest number of participants came from the two bases with the largest 17D presence, Lackland Air Force Base and Fort Meade.

We also recognized from our SME discussions that perspectives might differ in meaningful ways depending on the type of cyber work participants were involved in at the time. We therefore held discussions separately with participants from the four work types shown in Figure 2.1. Participants were asked to self-identify which group best described their current assignment.

Note that the "Other 17D or unknown" category includes discussions with people who self-identified as not being in an assignment belonging to one of the other groups (DoDIN, DCO, or OCO). These people were coded in our data as "other 17D." In a few cases, participants from multiple work types showed up at the same time and we interviewed them together; they were also grouped into the "Other 17D or unknown" category. Lastly, in a few instances, the group type was not articulated clearly on the audio recording, even if it may have been known at the time of the discussion. We recorded their group type in our data as "unknown" and for the purposes of the analysis grouped them with the "Other 17D or unknown" category. As can be seen in Figure 2.1, sample sizes ranged from 14 to 21.

In the few cases where we held group discussions, we separated CGOs from FGOs to ensure that participants felt comfortable speaking freely (senior officers thus did not need to be concerned about influencing junior officers with their comments, and junior officers were free to express themselves without fear of judgment or reprimand from their superiors). Thirty-four of the discussions were with CGOs, and 33 were with FGOs.[2]

---

[2] The type of grade group for one discussion was not recorded and therefore is not counted in the totals listed here.

Figure 2.1. Number of Discussions by Work Type

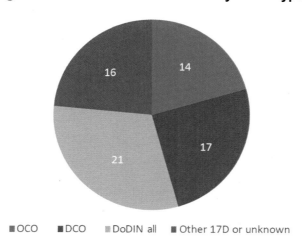

■ OCO   ■ DCO   ■ DoDIN all   ■ Other 17D or unknown

NOTE: DoDIN operations were defined as actions taken to design, build, configure, secure, operate, maintain, and sustain Department of Defense communications systems and networks in a way that creates and preserves data availability, integrity, confidentiality, as well as user/entity authentication and nonrepudiation.

At each base location, we reached out to the Air Force Reserve and Air National Guard 17D community for participation, but only a few reservists responded to our request. This was likely due to the fact that their numbers are generally small at these locations, and those that are stationed there most likely were not on base the days we were visiting and/or had conflicting civilian or military work commitments, making participation particularly inconvenient for them. In addition, it is important to note that we targeted members of the entire 17D community. Notably, some personnel serving in 17D billets are not themselves in the 17D career field; some are 62Es and 14Ns. We therefore welcomed participants who were serving in a 17D or 17S position, regardless of their actual career field designators. A few of these individuals responded and are included in our results.

The majority of focus groups lasted 90 minutes. Similar to the SME interviews, each RAND facilitator followed a number of introductory steps to ensure success with each focus group. Generally speaking, the process entailed (1) identifying the work type that best describes interviewees' current duty assignments; (2) collecting completed questionnaires from participants (if applicable); (3) providing five to ten minutes for questionnaire completion; (4) introduction of the research team and giving a synopsis of the study objectives; (5) review of informed consent; (6) informing participants of our intent to audio record; and (7) a bilateral exchange of background information.

We posed a different set of questions to focus group participants than to SMEs. For example, at the onset of our study we forecasted being able to get more nuanced information about desired behaviors, knowledge, skills, and abilities from 17D practitioners compared to senior leaders saddled with more managerial responsibilities. It turned out that we were correct, as a majority of DoDIN, DCO, and OCO respondents adeptly expressed what they thought made an ideal cyber operator. We also spent more time soliciting perspectives on the current status and direction of the 17D career field, asking CGOs and FGOs if their initial expectations were being met. The interview covered the following broad topics:

- drivers and obstacles to retention and recruiting
- current policy constraints to attracting and retaining 17Ds
- the organizational culture and leadership of the career field
- defining ideal behaviors, knowledge, skills, and abilities for 17Ds
- obstacles to getting the right behaviors, knowledge, skills, and abilities
- final thoughts and recommendations for the Air Force.

The Survey Administered to Interview Participants

As part of its focus group discussions, we administered a survey consisting of three types of questions. Several were open-ended questions, where respondents could provide qualitative, written feedback:

1. What do you like MOST about your job as a 17D?
2. What do you like LEAST about your job as a 17D?
3. What skills or qualities are critical in a 17D for ensuring mission success (or for preventing mission failure)?
4. Are there any other skills or qualities that 17Ds need? Why?
5. Is there anything else important about the 17D job or quality of life that we should know about?
6. Please provide any additional comments here.

There were also sixty Likert scale questions (such as questions scored on a scale ranging from 1 to 4 or 1 to 5), the majority of which came in response to the following two prompts: "How satisfied are you with the following aspects of the 17D job?" and "Thinking about your job in the 17D cyber community, how much do you agree with the following?" Some of the items were designed to be similar to items included in two other major military surveys—the 2015 Federal Employee Viewpoint Survey (FEVS) and the 2014 Status of Forces Survey (SOFS)—for purposes of benchmarking.[3]

---

[3] The FEVS is broken down into several demographic groups, such as the Department of Homeland Security, the Department of Agriculture, the Department of Defense, and the Department of Veterans Affairs. For our benchmarking purposes, we focused on the FEVS Department of Defense results from 72,919 officers and enlisted personnel combined. Sixteen of our questions were closely linked to the questions asked on the FEVS. The 2014 SOFS was administered to over 13,000 individuals across the services, but for the purposes of our study we focused on the results from 1,781 Air Force officers who ranged in rank from lieutenants to captains (960) or majors to colonels (821). Only a few of our survey items were aligned with the SOFS results. Members of the military are routinely asked to complete a variety of surveys. Knowing that this was the case, and having access to a number of surveys and survey results, we designed our survey to closely mirror or parallel available surveys when possible. Doing so allowed us to compare our 17D responses to that of other populations within the military as benchmarks.

The last portion of the survey asked for demographic data to provide information about the respondent's rank, job type, and training background. For the complete questionnaire, see Appendix D.

One hundred seven individuals provided written responses to our questionnaire. The means reported were weighted to reflect the distribution of personnel within the 17D community across the following ranks: first and second lieutenants, captains, majors, and lieutenant colonels.[4] Table 2.2 identifies our sample distribution, along with the distribution of officers across the larger 17D community. In total, two colonels completed our questionnaire. Rather than overweight this sample to reflect the distribution of colonels in the 17D community, we combined their survey results with those for the lieutenant colonels.[5] We then weighted our lieutenant colonel and colonel sample based on the distribution of lieutenant colonels in the 17D community.

Table 2.2. Rank Distribution of Participants Relative to the 17D Population

Rank	Sample Size	Sample Distribution	17D Officer Distribution
Lieutenants	28	26.2%	26.3%
Captains	41	38.3%	34.9%
Majors	29	27.1%	19.8%
Lieutenant colonel/colonel	9	8.4%	19.0% (lieutenant colonels only)

Interviews with Air Force Cyber SMEs

To identify key issues in the 17D community, we also sought the input of SMEs, each of whom brought a unique area of expertise to the discussion.[6] The names and titles of the SMEs are listed in Table 2.3.[7] As can be seen from the table, participants covered a diverse range of cyber perspectives. This included the 24th Air Force, or Air Forces Cyber (AFCYBER) commander, commanders at the Air Force cyber wing and group levels, the 17D career field manager, cyber leaders from Air Combat Command (ACC), the Air Force Reserve, Air Force Space Command (AFSPC), Joint Special Operations Command, the Pacific Air Forces,

---

[4] Rank distributions were calculated using Air Force personnel data.

[5] There were no obvious differences between the responses from colonels and lieutenant colonels.

[6] Our project sponsor provided us with an initial list of cyber SMEs to include in our interviews. A few additional SMEs were subsequently added based on suggestions from the initial SMEs.

[7] Prior to each interview, we provided SMEs an informed consent statement and the list of interview questions. At the start of the interview, we asked for permission to mention them as participants by name in our final report; all agreed.

Table 2.3. Air Force 17D Subject Matter Expert Interviewees

SMEs	Title or Office
Lt Col Jeffrey A. Blankenship	Special assistant for senior officer matters, Office of Information Dominance, and chief information officer (SAF/CIO A6)
Col John P. Boudreaux	Chief, Cyberspace Force Development Division (SAF/CIO A6) and 17D career field manager
Col Eric P. DeLange	Commander, 688th Cyberspace Wing
Col Brian Denman	Joint Staff J6, and commander, 688th Cyberspace Operations Group
Col Roberta D. Ernest	Chief, Operations Division (A6O), Headquarters, Air Force Reserve Command; interviewed with Lt Col Ryan W. Rasmussen, chief, Cyber Mission Development (A6O) and Maj Colin Williams (A6OD)
Col Glen M. Genove	Deputy director of Air and Cyberspace Operations (A3/6D) and chief information officer, director of Cyberspace Forces, Headquarters, Pacific Air Forces
Col Michelle L. Hayworth	Commander, 688th Cyberspace Wing
Col Bradley L. Pyburn	Commander, 67th Cyberspace Wing
Col Donovan L. Routsis	Deputy director of integrated air, space, cyberspace, and intelligence, surveillance, and reconnaissance operations, Air Force Space Command (A2/3/6)
Col Patrick S. Ryan	Reserve adviser to SAF/CIO A6
Col Chad D. Raduege	Commander, White House Communications Agency
Lt Col Samuel M. Snoddy	Air Force Personnel Center (DP2OA)
Col Jonathan A. Sutherland	Director of communications and chief information officer, Headquarters, United States Air Forces in Europe–Air Forces Africa
Col Jason K. Sutton	Air Combat Command (A6)
Col William C. Waynick II	Director, J-6, Joint Special Operations Command
Maj Gen Christopher P. Weggeman	Commander, 24th Air Force and Air Forces Cyber

Interviewed together:
    Col Steven J. Anderson
    Lt Col Billy E. Pope, Jr.
	Division chief, cyberspace strategy and policy senior executive officer, SAF/CIO A6

SAF/CIO A6, U.S. Air Forces in Europe–Air Forces Africa, and the White House.[8] In addition, we included the two individuals at the Air Force Personnel Center responsible for making assignment decisions for the 17D workforce (deciding which person to place in which open

---

[8] Several of those who were invited were also DT members. As described in Hanser et al., 2015, a DT is intended to address officer professional development and identify candidates for command positions, and is a team of people including a general officer, a career field manager, and others, that meet regularly to review an officer's performance assessments and career plans and compares these against requirements for the career field. Based on an officer's career plan, the DT recommends education or special duties and provides feedback to the officer and his or her supervisor.

position to satisfy both the career development needs of individuals and the mission requirements specified by commanders).

We held 17 interviews with 20 people, during which we asked a range of questions about important characteristics of personnel, drivers of and obstacles to retention and attrition, issues concerning leadership and work culture, and other obstacles to success within the cyber community. See Appendix E for a list of the SME discussion topics.

Interviews with Private-Sector SMEs

When it comes to finding out what might interest or dissuade people from considering a cyber officer job in the Air Force, the ideal population to target would be college graduates in the broader U.S. community, and especially those who might not already be interested. However, interviewing people who are not military employees requires Office of Management and Budget review, and approval can be a six-month process. That, unfortunately, was longer than we had available to us in this study. Nevertheless, targeting nine or fewer individuals is allowable.[9] We therefore invited several members of the private sector to participate, and a total of five graciously agreed to speak with us.

In total, we interviewed five professionals from a variety of civilian cyberindustry backgrounds. Although this number does not provide an adequate sample to represent the entire civilian cyberindustry, the individuals we interviewed provided meaningful insights for further research to investigate. The sample included one individual who works for a defense contractor and has worked closely with Air Force cyber personnel throughout his career; a professor at a large nonmilitary university who has taught hundreds of students in computer science and computer engineering departments; a cybersecurity researcher who has studied the field for two decades and has extensive experience working with government agencies; a professional who works as a program developer and data manager; and an applications developer. These individuals worked for companies with employees numbering from several hundred to many thousand.

We asked participants a series of questions to collect their views on what civilian cyber workforce professionals value in the companies and organizations they work for, their general perceptions of the Air Force cyber mission and capabilities, and potential best practices and recommendations that might be worthwhile for policymakers to examine in the future. Those questions can be found in Appendix F.

A study published in 2015 conducted in-depth interviews with senior cyber personnel at 26 companies chosen to have similar characteristics (e.g., size and functions) to the Air Force

---

[9] Although the research did not require Office of Management and Budget approval, it was still reviewed by the RAND Institutional Review Board to ensure adequate provisions for the protection of human subjects.

(Schmidt et al., 2015). RAND undertook that study with the explicit purpose of identifying commercial practices that might apply to the Air Force, and it therefore serves as a backdrop for the information we gleaned from our five interviews. The authors of that report suggest several areas where commercial practices are likely to be adaptable and beneficial to the Air Force. Specifically, companies in the commercial sector manage IT and information security as separate disciplines, and the Air Force should consider whether officers, enlisted members, and civilians should be similarly aligned with a single specialty. The authors also note that the Air Force information security workforce is 2.3 times smaller than what would be the corporate norm, and they describe the implications of corporate practice on which IT and information security functions to outsource, how to approach accessions, and the most efficient/effective ways to structure IT and information security organizations. Interested readers should consult this study, as it is the most applicable and in-depth resource available on how corporate practices could benefit the Air Force.

Our Approach to Reporting Results

We analyzed results from each of the three populations separately. What we found was overlap in the information that was obtained from all three sources. That is, all the topics and issues raised in the SME groups were echoed in the 17D workforce discussions, and the 17D discussions helped elaborate on the issues the SMEs raised. In addition, the 17D workforce interviews were conducted with a much larger sample, using a more structured discussion protocol, and included a written questionnaire. This allowed us a richer set of results relative to the SME discussions, which were less structured, shorter, and fewer in number. The comments provided by the private-sector SMEs also echoed the comments we heard from the other two groups, and were too few in number to allow anything but qualitative summaries of the high points of the discussions. Because both the SME results and the discussions with private-sector personnel were duplicative of the information provided by the 17D workforce, we opted to focus our discussion in this report of perspectives on the major drivers of 17D recruiting, retention and satisfaction solely on the findings from the 17D workforce interviews. With respect to the discussion about KSAOs in Chapter Three, we provide a combined summary of comments from both SMEs and 17D workforce.

Analysis of Qualitative Interview Comments

We analyzed participant comments by grouping them according to the types of themes that were repeated by multiple participants. SME and cyber workforce discussions were analyzed separately.

In the case of the SME discussions, we did not focus our results on a count of the numbers of participants mentioning each theme as the discussion topics varied depending on the area of expertise of the subject matter expert, and the sample sizes for the SME discussions are already

18

low. Instead we focused our SME discussion analysis efforts on producing a list of the range of topic areas the SMEs raised, along with example quotations for each.

To identify major themes and example quotations, we had one team member group each SME comment by theme or topic area. A second team member then reviewed those groupings to determine whether they agreed with the topic area themes and the placement of the SME comments. Categories of topics and placement of SME quotations were further adjusted and refined based on that review. The first coder then selected quotations illustrating the types of comments for inclusion in the write-up presented here.[10] Although we do not present a count of the numbers of SMEs mentioning a topic, it is worth noting that all themes discussed in our results were mentioned by more than one SME, and those described as top themes in the discussion were mentioned by several of them.

In analyzing our 17D workforce discussion results, we used a similar approach to establish our themes and topic areas. As a starting point for the list of themes, one researcher read through several of the discussion transcripts and generated a list of all the topic areas that were mentioned, along with a short description of the topic (including any examples of related terms or alternative wording used by the participants to refer to the same thing). Note that both positive and negative comments about a topic were included as separate categories, to the extent that they were mentioned (e.g., "STEM degree is needed," and "STEM degree is not needed"). A second researcher read through a new set of several transcripts and further refined the categories of topic areas and the descriptions. Together they came to an initial consensus on a starting list of topic areas or themes for coding. They then double-coded ten transcripts. During this process, the coding categories were further refined as new topics, and themes were identified. In addition, the category descriptions were revised further to ensure that any inconsistencies across coders were reconciled. Once they were reconciled, a third coder was trained, and all three coders coded the remainder of the transcripts, taking care to note any new topic area categories that were not already in the coding list.[11] The coders double-coded four additional transcripts for purposes of estimating coder agreement. On average, coders showed 93 percent agreement in their coding of those transcripts.[12]

---

[10] Comments that were not worded very clearly, that duplicated other better-worded examples, or that did not add much to the description already provided in the text were excluded for sake of brevity.

[11] Note that because the written responses were much shorter, a condensed version of the coding rubric (collapsing information into higher-level categories) was created and used for coding the written comments.

[12] This was estimated by first computing for each of the four transcripts the total number of coding categories receiving a 1 from both coders (where 1 indicates that a code is mentioned at least once in a discussion), divided by the total number of coding categories receiving a 1 by at least one of the coders. The results for each transcript were then averaged. This is a conservative estimate of reliability because it excludes from the numerator and denominator the categories that received a 0 from both coders (i.e., neither coder believed the topic was mentioned during the discussion). Using a less conservative approach, we calculated the total number of categories where the codes matched (i.e., both coded as 1 or both coded as 0) divided by the total number of coding categories that existed in our coding list. The estimate resulting from this approach was 98 percent agreement.

Lastly, it is important to note that in reporting results, we focused solely on counting whether a topic was mentioned at least once, not on the number of times it was mentioned across a single interview or survey. Our results do not double-count multiple mentions of a topic in a single discussion regardless of whether someone made the point multiple times, in multiple ways, or whether it was made by multiple individuals participating in the same group discussion. In other words, if a topic was mentioned, that discussion or survey was assigned a 1 in our coding of that topic, regardless of how many times it was mentioned. If it was not mentioned at any point in a discussion or a survey, it received a 0 in our coding of that topic.

3. Desired Characteristics of Cyber Personnel

Because the cyber domain encompasses many different functions and is rapidly evolving, forming a clear picture of the type of professional that might epitomize a successful cyber operator can be difficult (National Research Council, 2013). This chapter draws on prior research to describe the characteristics of successful cyber workforce professionals and how these characteristics apply to Air Force operations. We augment our findings from the research literature with views on desired characteristics of Air Force cyberspace professionals from our SME and 17D interview participants, which highlight not only many of the same characteristics but also potential differences particular to a military environment.

Existing Research on Desired Characteristics of Cyber Workforce Professionals

When analyzing the characteristics that workers need in order to perform a job, psychologists commonly discuss requirements in the areas of KSAOs. Differentiating characteristics in this way helps to distinguish between characteristics that are changeable, such as command of information and task performance (i.e., knowledge and skills, respectively), from the capacity to perform activities (abilities), which is thought to be more stable over time (Morgeson and Dierdorff, 2011). The "other" category serves to capture remaining characteristics that might be relevant, such as personality and motivation.

As a starting point for building a more complete picture of the ideal Air Force cyber operator, we examine KSAOs that prior studies have mentioned in the cyber workforce context. An important caveat when applying this information to the Air Force cyber workforce is that some of the taxonomies in the research literature encompass functions that do not overlap well with the primary career field of interest—17D cyberspace operations. Further, some studies do not clearly differentiate the emergent field of cybersecurity (which involves securing and defending an organization's IT systems from security breaches or other malicious attacks) from the general field of IT (which instead focuses on building, maintaining, and providing support for users of IT systems in an organization) in examining required KSAOs (Trippe et al., 2014). In addition, the KSAOs unique to military operations or the officer corps are likely absent from studies of general cyber workforce professionals (Suby, 2015). Still, KSAOs that existing studies have mentioned can provide a baseline for the types of characteristics associated with the cyber workforce field and are therefore discussed here in detail.

Table 3.1 provides a list of knowledge areas that prior studies have associated with the cyber workforce. As shown in Table 3.1, many of the knowledge areas identified in the literature are

Table 3.1. Knowledge Areas Needed for Cybersecurity and IT Workforce Professionals

Description	Linked Only to Cybersecurity	Source
Broad understanding of the security field	X	Suby, 2015
Awareness and understanding of the latest security threats	X	Suby, 2015
Technical knowledge (security packages, networks and network security components, firewall management skills, understanding security processes and controls)		Bagchi-Sen, Rao, and Upadhyaya, 2010; Conti and Raymond, 2011; Scott et al., 2010; Suby, 2015
Knowledge of relevant regulatory policy	X	Bagchi-Sen, Rao, and Upadhyaya, 2010; Suby, 2015
Security policy formulation and application	X	Suby, 2015
Legal knowledge	X	Bagchi-Sen, Rao, and Upadhyaya, 2010; Suby, 2015
Knowledge of risks, vulnerabilities, and threats	X	Suby, 2015
Enhanced understanding of security guidelines	X	Suby, 2015
Enhanced knowledge of multitenancy architecture	X	Suby, 2015
Knowledge of compliance issues	X	Suby, 2015
Knowledge of network protocols and standards		Trippe et al., 2014
Knowledge of telecommunication topologies		Trippe et al., 2014
Knowledge of file structure		Trippe et al., 2014
Knowledge of features and general uses of word processing software		Trippe et al., 2014
Knowledge of security methodologies for routing devices		Trippe et al., 2014
Knowledge of encryption and decryption methods		Trippe et al., 2014
Knowledge of basic language constructs		Trippe et al., 2014
Knowledge of database querying methods		Trippe et al., 2014
Knowledge of web-based data environments		Trippe et al., 2014
Understanding the differences between data formats		Trippe et al., 2014
Understanding the different numbering systems, such as hex and binary		Trippe et al., 2014

not unexpected. For example, both Suby (2015) and Trippe et al. (2014) mention the importance of relevant knowledge of networks and network security processes. Other areas, such as knowledge of regulatory policy, security policy, and the law, are less obvious and only indirectly related to technical computer knowledge.

Note that in this table (and in subsequent tables), we include a column indicating whether the sources focused just on cybersecurity professionals or whether they also made references to IT professionals.[1] Notably, the knowledge areas mentioned in studies looking solely at cybersecurity professionals are more likely to note areas that go beyond technical competence. For example, in the *2015 (ISC)² Global Information Security Workforce Study*, "broad understanding of the security field" was ranked highest in importance to success in information security, ahead of even "technical knowledge" (Suby, 2015, p. 24). Other research supports the importance of legal and regulatory knowledge to cybersecurity (Bagchi-Sen, Rao, and Upadhyaya, 2010), an area that is also of importance to cyberspace operations officers in the Air Force (Yannakogeorgos and Geis, 2016). Further, these auxiliary knowledge areas could be lacking in computer science curriculums, which is why others have noted that elite cybersecurity professionals are likely to emerge from diverse academic backgrounds and why distinct cybersecurity education programs are beginning to emerge (Brouse, 2015; Libicki, Senty, and Pollack, 2014).

The skill sets that are beginning to characterize the cyber workforce are listed in Table 3.2. The skills reflect many technical functions that are foundational to operating in the cyber domain, such as programming, database concepts, and software system development. Other skill areas, however, that might be less commonly associated with cyber include communication, leadership, and project management skills; in Suby (2015) communication skills, in particular, ranked highest in importance among the items in Table 3.2. These skills also happen to accord well with 17D duties and responsibilities, which include leadership functions (e.g., "Operates weapon system[s] and commands crew"), as well as responsibilities where project management and communication skills are essential (e.g., "Develops plans and policies, monitors operations, and advises commanders"). Finally, in a manifesto describing a new undergraduate degree program in "cyber security engineering," Brouse (2015) proposes a shift from focusing on reactive threat mitigation to proactive engineering of more secure systems. Skill areas such as architecture, security engineering, and risk assessment and management reflect this idea. The need for professionals who can design security systems and write safe code is also emphasized in Evans and Reeder (2010).

---

[1] The fact that certain knowledge areas are linked only to cybersecurity in previous reports does not necessarily mean that the area is not required for workers in IT, but rather that we did not find a study specifically citing the area as required for IT. Attempting to contrast cyber and IT in this way is imperfect, as it is subject to the particular questions that past researchers have decided to study.

The primary source for distinct abilities that are necessary for cyber workforce professionals is Trippe et al. (2014), which documents results from several studies initiated by the Air Force with the goal of developing a cyber and information/communications technology literacy test that could be used for screening. The authors reviewed existing KSAOs for their target population (enlisted cyber/IT operators) and refined them with interviews with SMEs and an online survey. Table 3.2 lists the 11 nonphysical abilities mentioned in the report. The necessary traits include several types of cognitive reasoning and communication abilities, and the authors note that written comprehension, advanced written comprehension, written expression, and oral comprehension held four of the top five importance ratings in the SME survey results. It is also noteworthy that Trippe et al. identified originality as an ability linked to cybersecurity, and several of the other characteristics summarized in the next section highlight related areas. In total, the existing work potentially points to a distinct mix of cognitive abilities as being most predictive of success in the cyber field.

Table 3.2. Skill and Ability Areas Needed for Cybersecurity and IT Workforce Professionals

Description	Linked Only to Cybersecurity and IT	Source
Skill Areas		
Communication skills		Bagchi-Sen, Rao, and Upadhyaya, 2010; LeClair, Abraham, and Shih, 2013; Suby, 2015
Leadership skills		Bagchi-Sen, Rao, and Upadhyaya, 2010; LeClair, Abraham, and Shih, 2013; Suby, 2015
Project management skills	X	LeClair, Abraham, and Shih, 2013; Suby, 2015
Business management skills	X	Bagchi-Sen, Rao, and Upadhyaya, 2010; Suby, 2015
Risk assessment and management	X	Suby, 2015
Incident investigation and response	X	Suby, 2015
Governance, risk management, and compliance	X	Suby, 2015
Analytical skills	X	LeClair, Abraham, and Shih, 2013; Suby, 2015
Architecture	X	LeClair, Abraham, and Shih, 2013; Suby, 2015
Information systems and security operations management	X	Suby, 2015
Virtualization	X	Suby, 2015
Platform or technology specific skills	X	Suby, 2015

Description	Linked Only to Cybersecurity and IT	Source
Business and business development skills	X	Suby, 2015
Engineering	X	Suby, 2015
Data administration and management	X	Suby, 2015
Software system development	X	Suby, 2015
Acquisition/procurement (supply chain)	X	Suby, 2015
Application of security controls to cloud environments	X	Suby, 2015
Security engineering	X	LeClair, Abraham, and Shih, 2013; Suby, 2015
Service-level agreement skills	X	Suby, 2015
Audit	X	Suby, 2015
Data and information–centric approaches to security	X	Suby, 2015
Criminal psychology	X	LeClair, Abraham, and Shih, 2013
Technical writing	X	LeClair, Abraham, and Shih, 2013
Teamwork	X	LeClair, Abraham, and Shih, 2013; Yannakogeorgos and Geis, 2016.
Human Computer Interaction	X	LeClair, Abraham, and Shih, 2013
Data communications and networking	X	LeClair, Abraham, and Shih, 2013
Database concepts	X	LeClair, Abraham, and Shih, 2013
Programming	X	LeClair, Abraham, and Shih, 2013
Operating systems	X	LeClair, Abraham, and Shih, 2013
Investigation and forensic analysis to detect intruders	X	Bagchi-Sen, Rao, and Upadhyaya, 2010
Information security support skills	X	Bagchi-Sen, Rao, and Upadhyaya, 2010
Critical thinking	X	Yannakogeorgos and Geis, 2016
Ability Areas		
Verbal reasoning		Trippe et al., 2014
Nonverbal reasoning		Trippe et al., 2014
Mathematical reasoning		Trippe et al., 2014
Problem sensitivity		Trippe et al., 2014
Originality		Trippe et al., 2014
Information ordering		Trippe et al., 2014
Written communication		Trippe et al., 2014
Oral comprehension		Trippe et al., 2014

Description	Linked Only to Cybersecurity and IT	Source
Perceptual speed		Trippe et al., 2014
Advanced written comprehension		Trippe et al., 2014
Written expression		Trippe et al., 2014

Finally, Table 3.3 lists several other characteristics that came up in the studies that we reviewed. The results in Suby (2015) suggest that education levels are rising in the cybersecurity field, and they mention possessing an information security degree as a potentially important characteristic. However, other studies partly downplay the importance of education credentials in the short term and instead highlight noncognitive characteristics, such as creativity and independence, as being important to success in the cyber field. For instance, possessing an information security degree ranked last in importance to success among the items in Suby (2015), and Libicki, Senty, and Pollack state that several interviewees thought "deep curiosity and drive to understand how things work" were better indicators of cyber talent than education credentials (2014, p. 63). Drawing on the logic in the major recommendation of the National Research Council (2013), credentials might be less useful as skill indicators, while the knowledge and skill requirements of the field are not stable. Further, Yannakogeorgos and Geis (2016) state that their expert interviews indicated that good hackers are "autodidactic" (i.e., self-teaching), which accords with intuition given the challenge of keeping pace in such a rapidly evolving field.

Table 3.3. Other Qualities Needed for Cybersecurity and IT Workforce Professionals

Description	Linked Only to Cybersecurity	Source
Higher degree	X	Suby, 2015
Possession of an information security degree	X	Suby, 2015
Creativity	X	Conti and Raymond, 2011
Independence	X	Conti and Raymond, 2011
Intense curiosity with how things work (and can be made to fail)	X	Libicki, Senty, and Pollack, 2014
Autodidactism	X	Yannakogeorgos and Geis, 2016

Synthesizing the KSAOs from the existing studies of the cyber workforce field, one can see the beginnings of a coherent picture of a successful cybersecurity operator. Successful operators need a body of technical knowledge of computers and networks, no doubt, but they also need knowledge in auxiliary areas such a legal and regulatory policy. Necessary skills include forensic analysis—that is, finding and eliminating threats and vulnerabilities—but also the ability to design robust and secure IT systems. Finally, the ideal cyberspace operator would possess a distinct set of cognitive abilities, but also noncognitive traits such as intense curiosity that might drive one to operate at the high level needed to counter the most sophisticated cyber adversaries.

Existing Research on Desired Characteristics in the Air Force Cyber Workforce

At times, the prevailing narrative of the cyber workforce crisis creates the impression that all organizational players are vying for the same talent to enable them to solve the same sorts of problems of network vulnerability. This narrative contains some truth, but it also glosses over the ways in which the national security cyber mission differs from mere cybersecurity.

There is demand in both the civilian and national security sectors for the design, security, and maintenance of IT systems. Joint doctrine labels this function DoDIN Operations, and defines it as "actions taken to design, build, configure, secure, operate, maintain, and sustain DoD [Department of Defense] communications systems and networks in a way that creates and preserves data availability, integrity, confidentiality, as well as user/entity authentication and non-repudiation" (Joint Chiefs of Staff, 2013). As with national security operations in domains other than cyberspace, however, cyberspace operations include defensive and offensive functions that engage and counter adversaries directly. Thus, in addition to defending DoD networks, Air Force cyber operators must supply capabilities in the realms of intelligence, surveillance, and reconnaissance, operational preparation of the environment (i.e., other activities that enable military operations), and cyberspace attack (i.e., using cyber to engage military targets). In sum, the broader national security cyber mission necessarily entails additional, unique KSAOs.

The best information available on KSAOs unique to Air Force cyber operations comes from Scott et al. (2010), a pioneering study that examined positions that contributed to cyber capabilities prior to the introduction of the 17D career field and the start-up of the cyber training pipeline. This study examined these "cyber-hybrid" officers by specialty, and collected information on the areas where the officer skill sets needed to be augmented by other KSAOs in order to fulfill cyber missions (see Table 3.4). Some of these areas echo the KSAOs of the civilian sector, but most areas require familiarity with concepts and capabilities that are proprietary to DoD. While both civilian and national security cyber operators need knowledge of cyberthreats, for example, one is unlikely to become familiar with network warfare operations and computer network exploitation tools and weapons apart from working at DoD or the intelligence community. Further, these Air Force cyber officer KSAOs highlight the need for familiarity with the electromagnetic spectrum. Although the electromagnetic spectrum is certainly relevant to civilian applications, military operations involve electromagnetic complexity in a much greater magnitude.

27

Table 3.4. Distinctive KSAOs of Cyber Officers

Knowledge, Skill, or Ability Area	Associated Specialty Areas
Electronic warfare	Rated
Information operations	Rated, space/missile, engineering/ science, communications/computer science
Intelligence	Space/missile, communications/computer science
Network analysis	Intelligence
Cyber threats	Intelligence, communications/computer science
Hacking methodology	Intelligence
Computer network exploitation tools/weapons	Intelligence
Electromagnetic spectrum knowledge	Engineering/science, communications/computer science
Network warfare operations	Communications/computer science, acquisition
Influence operations	Clinical psychology

SOURCE: Scott et al., 2010.

Our Interview Findings on the Necessary Attributes of Cyber Personnel

As explained in Chapter Two, to build on KSAOs identified in the literature, we asked SMEs in the Air Force and members of the 17D workforce to identify, from their perspective within the military environment, the skills needed for ensuring mission success within the 17D community.

As a reminder, we analyzed participant comments by grouping them according to the types of themes that were repeated by multiple participants. SME and cyber workforce discussions were analyzed separately. In the case of the SME discussions, we do not present a count of the numbers of participants mentioning each theme, as only a subset of the discussions focused on addressing this question and the sample sizes for SMEs are already low. Instead we present in this chapter a list of the KSAO themes or topic areas they raised along with example quotations for each.

The results showed that the KSAOs mentioned by our SMEs and our 17D workforce participants were quite similar. Starting first with the 17D workforce findings, Figure 3.1 shows the types of qualities that were raised during our discussion with members of the 17D community, broken up by work group.[2] As shown in the figure, the top KSAO topic areas included technical, leadership, and problem solving/critical thinking skills. All three were viewed

---

[2] As a reminder, some discussions were held with a single individual, whereas others were held with multiple participants at once in a focus group format. The estimates provided in the figure therefore show the percentage of discussions where the KSAO was mentioned, not the number of individuals who mentioned it. This means that while it was not the case that a single individual would express an opposite sentiment, it was possible for opposite sentiments to be expressed in one focus group by two different people. In addition, note that these results are unweighted, as it does not make sense to use individual-level population estimates to correct responses that include group-level discussion information, as is the case here.

Figure 3.1. Ideal Qualities for a 17D, as Described During the Interviews

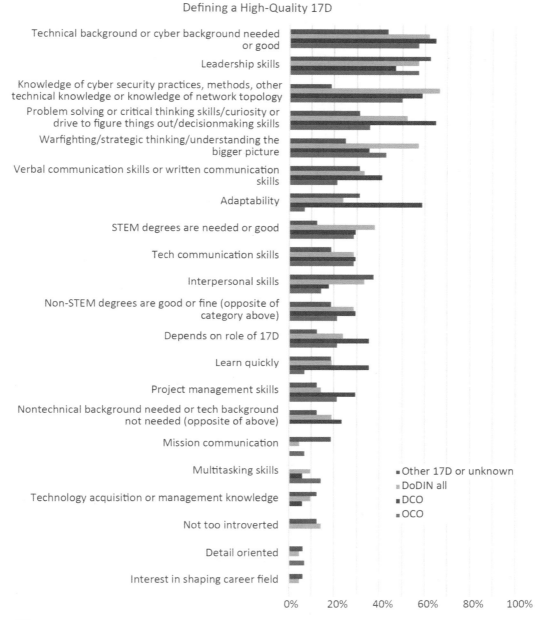

Defining a High-Quality 17D

Legend: Other 17D or unknown · DoDIN all · DCO · OCO

NOTE: *n* = 70.

by our participants as important qualities for 17Ds to have, and they were frequently the first KSAOs mentioned in the discussion. The following is an example:

> Leadership, leadership, leadership. Eighty to 90 percent of an officer's job is leading, even a second lieutenant at the tactical level must be a leader. I can hire civilians and contractors to do our keyboard stuff if that's all we care about. But a 17D is a military officer and must see themselves as an officer first and a 17D second.

Although the results of the 17D workforce discussions and the SME discussions uncovered a similar list of KSAOs, the SME comments about several of the most frequently mentioned topic areas in Figure 3.1 offered a number of useful insights into why those KSAOs define a high-quality 17D. We therefore include examples of the comments provided by the SMEs for those same topics in the remainder of this section.

Technical Expertise, Strong Leadership, and the "Warfighting Mind-Set" Were Cited as Pivotal to Cyber Success

When asked about what kinds of KSAOs the Air Force should be seeking in cyber personnel, participants stressed the importance of technical aptitude and expertise. Aptitude would enable incoming recruits to be capably trained on how to understand the technical landscape of the position if they do not have prior knowledge or training:

> I think [for] success at the joint level, we need to have people with exceptional technical skills that can execute those missions and develop tool sets they can take down range.

> I don't mind emphasizing the technical, but I don't think that's a limitation by anybody coming into our career field. . . . When you talk about those key KSAOs, you're talking about an ideal end state that I don't think has to be achieved.

> If you succeeded with that, it wasn't because you had a science background, it's because you could logically step through a process and understand what was being shown to you and then put this big amorphous puzzle together in your mind and then, finally, go, "Okay, what am I missing here?"

> You have to have technical abilities and technical understanding.

Some participants also spoke to leadership abilities—the ability to move out and have people be willing to follow you:

> I don't think what defines the success of a 17D is really any different than what defines the success of a general officer. Leadership ability, understanding of the mission and understanding of how to pull together your unique skill sets from whatever your job is for the execution of a mission, taking care of your personnel—whether that's fellow officers, enlisted or civilian contractors—integrating those into a cohesive team.

> The leadership skills, the interpersonal relationship skills, the ability to work under duress, the ability to work under challenging conditions, the ability to work with people with different backgrounds.

> There's that understanding that we need thinkers and we need leaders. We will teach you the Air Force requirements from a technical standpoint, experience will be received, and you will be developed over time.

Also, as shown in Figure 3.1, among the top most common themes was that people really need a "warfighting mind-set," an understanding of the mission, how their work fits into the mission, and an appreciation for the bigger picture context. For example:

> I think it's the warfighter mind-set, and I'm really thinking of what it takes to make a mission occur. . . . It's a mind-set of competence, it's a mind-set of methods for how we do things. There's been a lot of "operationalization" by introducing weapons programs, introducing tactics.

> I look for three elements: leadership, then technical acumen, the last is the warfighting competency, which takes these capabilities and employs them to an adversary offensively or defensively and understand[s] how they aid the mission.

> Are we IT professionals first or warfighters first? We need to see ourselves as warfighters first and provide the necessary skills, and we can defend the F-22 from cyberattacks.

> That's what we do. We build combat warfighters to hunt down and destroy America's enemies.

This topic (having a strategic and operational understanding of the bigger picture) was one area that received extended discussion during the 17D workforce interviews as an area where people felt the community was particularly weak and in need of improvement.

Critical Thinking and Communication Skills Were Also Frequently Cited as Critical

Critical thinking, creativity, continuous learning, and learning quickly also came up frequently in discussions, as cybertechnology is constantly changing. For example, one participant referred to a need for the "passion to learn as much as they can and the willingness to get back up after failing" and the "ability to understand complex problems and be able to think outside the box." Another offered a similar statement:

> Critical thinking and being able to apply that thinking to new situations. Things are constantly changing; thus, being able to wrap your mind around new ideas and new situations is critical. [A] willingness to fail, learn from failing, trying new things.

Participants also noted the importance of communication (both written and oral). "Bridging the gap between technical and functional (mission impact) is critical, requiring balanced knowledge of both system and mission to make effective decisions," is what one survey respondent had to say. In the case of cyber, communication was viewed as more critical than in other jobs because cyber is so technical that leadership struggles to understand it (they may not truly appreciate how useful it can be to the mission, how risky or not risky various actions can be, etc.). One survey response stated it this way:

> A difficult, though important, skill I think 17Ds need is the ability to relay technical information into actionable information for leadership decisions. I think many times we are either technically good but unable to communicate well with leadership, or vice versa. The balance is important.

As a result, participants expressed the belief that to move the Air Force's cyber capability forward, people within the 17D community need to be able to translate their technical cyber work into lay terms and articulate clearly the pros and cons of various courses of action to leadership.

This topic of being good at communicating with various stakeholders was another area that received extended discussion during the 17D workforce interviews as an area where people felt the community was particularly weak and in need of improvement.

Mixed Opinions on the Ideal Educational Degree for Cyber Recruits

Comments from some SMEs were split on whether or not the Air Force should prioritize STEM degrees over other nontechnical, liberal arts degrees. Some SMEs stated that the current value statement from the Air Force is STEM, given the benefit of recruiting personnel who are already proven to understand the technical demands of the profession. These SMEs stated:

> Right now, the value statement is the STEM career field.

> We're looking for STEM folks. We're thinking of partnering with the CyberPatriot Program for recruiting. We're looking for folks with these backgrounds walking in the door.

> One of the requirements that we arbitrarily put out there for 17Ds is that we want 90 percent to have a STEM degree. Currently, about 50 percent of new recruits are those folks. I don't believe that a geologist—which is a STEM, that's a science—has anything to do with whether you can handle yourself on a network. It just proves you have a calculating mind, can define programs, and move through things with rigor. That's not always what you need when you're trying to creatively look at this kind of amorphous thing that we call cyber.

> One of the things we have done as a career field is want 80 to 90 percent STEM degrees, but we are making about 50 to 60 percent. We need to develop a standardized test to see what their capability is to fulfill those roles.

Statements from SMEs who seemed to lean toward a mixture of degrees suggested that although the STEM mission statement exists, the Air Force may benefit from being open-minded, because different degrees offer varying perspectives. Several SMEs said:

> It's easy for us to say STEM, especially computer science, computer engineering, or cyberspace security. . . . But sometimes the diversity in thought is important. We can take a person with a liberal arts background and give them technical training; their thought process, especially on the offensive side, is powerful. The large number we look at, maybe 60 to 70 percent, should be STEM. But we should still leave room for highly educated liberal arts backgrounds with the undergraduate cyber training. I think that's powerful. I wouldn't say 100 percent STEM.

> There is no single thread of success attached to which degree they have. I think if we did look, we'd probably find biology or sociology majors are doing the best. I don't think we need to limit them.

We are seeing that for operations, the employment of cyberoperations to achieve military goals, we may not always want exclusively STEM majors. We may want to have folks that can think outside the box or rationalize in a different way and bring different pieces of the puzzle together and integrate that while using a cyber solution.

I'm a social science type. I see things a little bit different than the electrical engineer. I typically look at a blank piece of paper opposed to someone with a more structured line of thinking that may already have an algorithm to look at problems. Not to say one is bad and one is good, but the two need to coexist and leverage off of one another. I think that's where that balance, the nuance, needs to come into play.

This concern regarding diversity of thought being potentially beneficial is not unique to the cyber workforce in our study. In fact, a well-established theory known as the attraction-selection-attrition model (for an overview, see Schneider, Goldstein, and Smith, 1995) argues that the process of attracting, selecting, and retaining people with a narrow set of characteristics can potentially lead to a more homogeneous workforce over time, which can in turn stifle creativity and ingenuity and prevent legitimate alternative views from being heard. In this way, researchers agree that good arguments can be made for ensuring that some diversity of backgrounds is maintained and fostered in any workforce.[3]

Potential Differences in KSAOs Needed in Private-Sector Versus Military Cyber Workers

A comparison of the KSAOs identified in the research literature to those described by our Air Force interview participants shows a great deal of overlap (e.g., leadership, communication, critical thinking, and technical expertise are common to both lists). Consistent with this finding, some SMEs who talked with us about the KSAOs they look for in recruits mentioned that, for the most part, there is not much difference in necessary skill sets between the military and civilian sectors. As one SME said, "They would be the same. The criteria involved in recruiting would be the same." Although there are many similarities in the labels given to the KSAOs cited, the underlying construct may differ markedly between the private sector and military environments. That is, the meaning of leadership and communication in the military cyber context may be distinct. The example comments provided here are intended to help provide concrete examples of that meaning.

Other comments from SMEs and the 17D workforce emphasized important differences between the civilian and military sector in that the military performs offensive operations. For

---

[3] Here the type of diversity alluded to is that of educational specialty (including people with degrees other than computer science or engineering, or degrees outside of STEM), not that of race or gender diversity. Race or gender diversity may be of interest as well, but was not a target of the discussion in our focus groups.

example, one participant stated, "I think the biggest difference from the civilian world is the fact we are doing offensive operations. We're all doing the same things in terms of cybersecurity, but the main difference with us is that we attack our adversaries." Consistent with this view, in comparing the KSAOs, the one quality that stands out as unique to the Air Force cyber context is the "warfighting mind-set" (including the understanding of the mission, how one's work fits into that mission, and an appreciation for the bigger picture).

Additional Research Measuring Links to Effectiveness Could Be Beneficial

While it is true that the private-sector research literature is rich with descriptions of the KSAOs needed on the job, and that the additional information gleaned from our interviews suggests a number of other KSAOs might be relevant for Air Force cyber officers, more research on this topic could be beneficial. More specifically, it is important to note that the characteristics of successful cyber operators identified in this study and elsewhere are based largely on perceptions of cyber SMEs and job incumbents. Little research has been done linking those KSAOs to actual performance of cyber operators and, in this case, cyber officers, on the job.

To explain further, studies like ours have taken an important first step in linking KSAOs to the job by collecting job incumbent and SME perceptions of what is needed for effective performance, but further steps to confirm and supplement this information could be worthwhile. For example, a better understanding of the relative impact of each of these KSAOs in predicting effectiveness would be helpful for prioritizing personnel training, education, and screening efforts in a resource-constrained environment. In addition, while job incumbent and SME perceptions are often taken as accurate assessments of what is needed to be successful (collecting job incumbent perceptions is a common approach to job analysis), the accuracy of such perceptions is not guaranteed. Examinations of the direct relationship between these KSAOs and effectiveness can therefore help further validate this information.

Several research efforts have sought to explore relationships between various cyber aptitudes and cyber performance for purposes of screening personnel prior to entry into technical training (Tripp et al. 2014; Waage and Morris, 2015). This research is still in its infancy, however, and it does not address the impacts of the many other KSAOs that have been discussed in this chapter. As such, it is important to note that research measuring the magnitude of the relationship between on-the-job effectiveness and the range of other KSAOs discussed in this chapter could provide useful additional insights.

4. Insights from the Air Force Cyber Workforce on Recruiting and Retention

It is generally well accepted that pay is not the only driver of retention in the workplace; job satisfaction also plays an important role (Griffeth, Hom, and Gaertner, 2000). In addition, recent research on best practices for retention within the private sector suggests that fostering job satisfaction is one of the primary tools that private-sector organizations leverage to retain in-demand cyber personnel (Schmidt et al., 2015). It is also well established that perceptions of the job and other aspects of the organization and work environment are also likely drivers of an individual's choice about which occupations or organizations to pursue during his or her job search (Kristof-Brown, Zimmerman, and Johnson, 2005; Schneider, Goldstein, and Smith, 1995).[1]

With this in mind, we sought to better understand people's attitudes toward the Air Force's cyber officer occupation (including their satisfaction with various aspects of the work and the Air Force's management of the cyber workforce). We amassed a wealth of qualitative information from the three interview sources (Air Force SMEs, private-sector SMEs, and 17D workforce job incumbents), all of which is useful in informing policies and practices related to recruiting and retention within the Air Force's cyber workforce. Each group brought useful perspectives and insights to the discussion. However, we were able to expand on those insights in much greater detail during our interviews with and through the survey administered to the 17D workforce. We therefore focus our discussion here on the results from those 17D interviews. Insights from the Air Force and private-sector SMEs were similar.

The remainder of this chapter discusses the quantitative and qualitative findings from those interviews. The first half of the discussion focuses on our quantitative survey results (the ratings of satisfaction and other aspects of the job). That section starts with a discussion of the results from the global satisfaction items. Results from the more specific satisfaction items (those asking about specific aspects of how the 17D workforce is managed, and other aspects of the 17D work life) are described next. Following that, we present results for three additional items (one on permeable service, one on having the option of serving in a technical track, and one on likelihood of leaving the service).

Throughout that discussion of results, we note several instances where items are identical to those administered on the 2014 SOFS. In those cases, we report whether the responses were different from those observed for the Air Force officers as a whole on the 2014 SOFS. In a

---

[1] For a short overview of insights on recruiting and retaining a skilled cyber workforce from the existing published research literature, see Appendix B.

separate section after that discussion, we also compare several results to similar items administered on the FEVS, again noting where responses were statistically significantly different. In the final section of quantitative survey results we explore whether there are statistically significant differences in responses by work type or by grade group (FGO versus CGO).

The latter half of the chapter focuses on our qualitative results from the survey and the focus group and interview discussions. We begin by presenting a figure illustrating the range of themes that were offered in response to the open-ended survey items asking what participants liked most and least about their jobs, and reporting the number of participants mentioning each theme.[2] Along with the figure, we present examples of the write-in comments on the survey and the oral comments offered during the interview and focus group discussions that illustrate each theme. In the remaining three sections, we describe the criticisms of training that were raised during the discussions, additional comments offered during the discussions about other concerns or sources of dissatisfaction, and participants' ideas or suggestions for how to improve recruiting or retention.

Ratings of Satisfaction and Other Aspects of the Job

Satisfaction with Various Aspects of the 17D Job

The survey we administered included two global questions about satisfaction: "How satisfied are you with your current duty assignment" and "How satisfied are you with your career in general as a 17D?" Figure 4.1 summarizes the overall responses to these questions. As can be seen in the figure, on average, most individuals in our sample are satisfied with both their duty assignment and career. In addition, when asked whether they would decide to stay on active duty if given the chance to leave, the average response was a 2.34, where 2 represented the response "Likely" and 3 represented "Neither likely nor unlikely."

---

[2] We conducted a detailed coding analysis of the focus group discussion transcripts, in addition to the survey write-in responses. However, the results of the focus group coding echoed the findings from the survey that are presented later in this chapter—that is, they produced the same themes and the same general rank ordering of themes. As such, presenting both would be largely redundant. Given that the survey findings included a larger sample size and are attributable to individuals, whereas the discussions were not (recall that some interviews were held as group discussions, with multiple participants contributing to the discussion), we favored the survey coding counts for inclusion here. The only meaningful difference between the discussion coding and the survey write-in response coding was the frequency of a topic being raised—that is, participants often brought up topics during discussion that they had not included in their written responses. Because of these frequency differences existing between the survey and discussion comments, we also report general rates of frequency with which the topic was mentioned in the oral discussion in our text description of those qualitative results.

Figure 4.1. Global Job Satisfaction Ratings

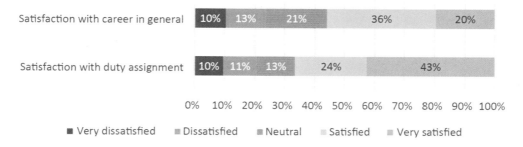

NOTE: *n* = 107.

Respondents were asked 27 follow-up questions about their satisfaction with different aspects of the 17D job. Figure 4.2 shows the average responses to these questions, presenting several noteworthy results. First, the average response for many of these satisfaction-based questions was around 3.0 or higher. This would further indicate that the average cyber operator is satisfied with many aspects of his or her career. However, for nine questions the average response was below 3.0, and for 14 of the 27 questions the 95 percent confidence interval included a range of values below 3.0. Second, it is worth noting that respondents are clearly dissatisfied on average with prospects for retaining members of the community. As shown in Table 4.1, almost 30 percent of our respondents were very dissatisfied with this aspect of the 17D community.

Table 4.1. 17D Satisfaction with Retention

	Very Dissatisfied	Dissatisfied	Neutral	Satisfied	Very Satisfied
Satisfaction with 17D retention	29%	27%	31%	10%	3%

NOTE: Item prompt was "How satisfied are you with the following aspects of the 17D job?" The item referenced here is "Retention of 17Ds."

Third, job security topped the list of items from Figure 4.2. Notably, the 2014 SOFS asked the same question. In comparison, however, 17Ds satisfaction was significantly higher ($p < .0001$). On the same 1 to 5 scale, Air Force officers on the SOFS had an average response of 3.7 across grade groups, whereas 17Ds had an average of 4.3. In other words, 17Ds show a higher-than-average rate of satisfaction with job security than do other Air Force officers.

Two other aspects of the 17D job for which respondents expressed large degrees of satisfaction were retirement pay and civilian job opportunities; satisfaction with pay/allowances was not far behind, with an average of 3.9. The 2014 SOFS asked a similar question about overall compensation; Air Force officer results were not statistically different (the average across grades was 4.1).

37

Figure 4.2. Satisfaction with Key Aspects of the 17D Job

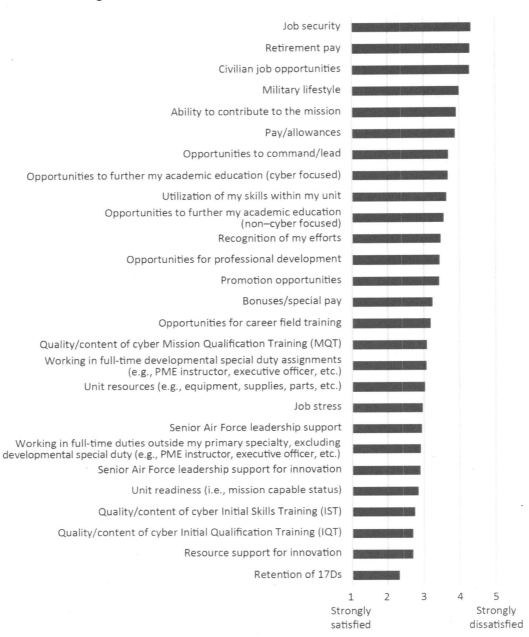

Satisfaction with bonuses and special pay, however, was not particularly positive (no comparable item was asked on the SOFS). Personnel were slightly more satisfied with promotion opportunities, with more than half of respondents saying they were "Satisfied" or "Very satisfied." Only around 30 percent expressed satisfaction with the amount of stress associated with their job.

Participants were asked about satisfaction with the military lifestyle, and the results showed that, on average, participants were satisfied with this aspect of their job. This response is not statistically different from the response to the 2014 SOFS question on individual satisfaction with "military values, lifestyle, and tradition" (averaging around 4.0 across the two officer grade groups), suggesting that 17Ds have statistically the same satisfaction with the military lifestyle as does the rest of the Air Force officer corps.

The 2014 SOFS also asked respondents their satisfaction with training and professional development opportunities. The average response to this question from Air Force officers across all ranks was a 3.5. Our survey asked a similar question in two parts: First, respondents were asked their satisfaction with career field training opportunities; second, they were asked about professional development opportunities. In regard to career field training, the average response was 3.2; for professional development, it was 3.5. The difference between these results and the results of the 2015 SOFS are not statistically significant.

Although responses about opportunities for career field training and professional development were not negative and not noticeably different from those of officers on the SOFS, responses about quality and content of initial qualification training and initial skills training told a slightly different story. This issue of dissatisfaction with training also came up at length in the discussions and the written comments; those criticisms are discussed later in this chapter.

Level of Agreement with Statements about Key Aspects of the 17D Job

Respondents were asked 25 subquestions under the prompt, "Thinking about your job in the 17D cyber community, how much do you agree with the following?" Possible responses ranged from 1, "Strongly disagree," to 5, "Strongly agree." Mean responses on those items are shown in Figure 4.3.

One of the most notable findings is how low the average agreement was with the item about perceived difficulty finding a job. In fact, 75 percent of respondents strongly disagreed that they would have difficulty finding a job if they left the military. These responses mirror the high satisfaction with civilian job opportunities shown in Figure 4.2. Of respondents, 27 percent agreed and 52 percent strongly agreed they were satisfied with the civilian job opportunities. The 2014 SOFS asked respondents the same question about difficulty finding a job if they left the military; responses were not statistically significantly different.

Two of the highest levels of agreement were related to how individuals feel about the work they do. Responses included "The work I do is important" and "I like the kind of work I do," with both items having average values of 3.8. Both items are discussed further in the section that follows. With respect to the question "I find real enjoyment in my work," participants gave slightly lower responses; however, the difference was not statistically significant. In addition, the results were not statistically different from the Air Force officer results on the 2014 SOFS, which included a question about satisfaction with the "amount of enjoyment from your job," for which the average response was 3.7.

Figure 4.3. Levels of Agreement with Additional Statements about the 17D Job

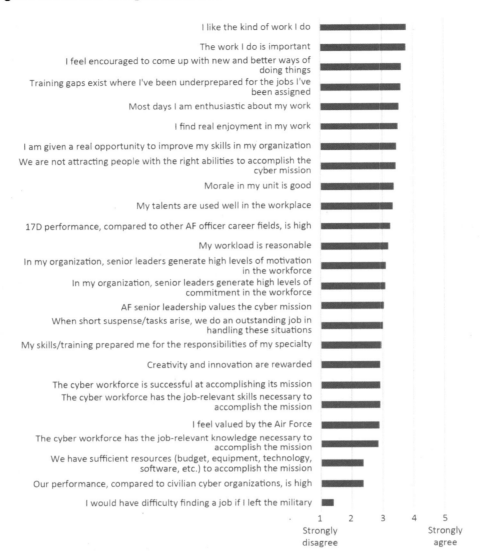

Although, on average, responses to these items were positive, it is also worth noting that a sizable percentage of individuals still disagreed or strongly disagreed with the items (ranging from 18 percent on "I like the kind of work I do" to 21 percent on "I find real enjoyment in my work").

In total, about one-third of respondents agreed or strongly agreed that they felt valued by the Air Force, roughly another third felt neutral on the subject, and the final third disagreed or strongly disagreed.

Several of the items listed in Figure 4.3 were similar or identical to items presented on the 2015 FEVS. Benchmark comparisons to the FEVS results are discussed in a separate section later in this chapter.

Additional Survey Questions

In addition to the set of questions concerning 17D agreement with different aspects of their career, respondents were asked two questions about their career goals. Table 4.2 highlights the results.

Table 4.2. 17D Career Goals

	N	Average Response	95% Confidence Interval (Lower)	95% Confidence Interval (Upper)
If you were given the option for permeable service among the regular Air Force and Air Reserve component, would you have accepted a longer service obligation upon your initial entry into the 17D career field?	105	2.82	2.56	3.07
If you were offered the opportunity to choose a cyber technical track, assuming equivalent pay/benefits, how would it influence your decision regarding remaining in the active duty Air Force?	105	3.54	3.33	3.76

The question concerning the option for permeable service ranged from 1, "Definitely," to 5, "Definitely not." The average response of 2.8 shows that 17Ds are largely unsure if they would be willing to accept a longer commitment in exchange for permeable service. However, the responses to the question about a technical track were much less unsure. The available options to that question ranged from 1, "Strongly influenced to leave," to 5, "Strongly influenced to stay." In total, 43 percent of respondents said that a technical track would influence or strongly influence them, whereas 45 percent felt that it would not make an impact on their decision to stay or leave.

Respondents were also asked two additional questions; one about their own careers, and one about the career field. The first question was, "Suppose that you have to decide whether to stay on active duty. Assuming you could stay, how likely is it that you would choose to do so?" On a scale ranging from 1, "Very unlikely," to 5, "Very likely," the average response by our 17D participants was a 3.6.[3] Responses to the same 2014 SOFS item was statistically significantly higher, at 3.8. As shown in Figure 4.4, approximately twice as many 17Ds respond that they are very unlikely to stay when compared to SOFS officers. Moreover, almost 27 percent of the 17D community respondents said it was unlikely or very unlikely that they would choose to stay if given the chance to leave.

---

[3] Note that this item is coded in the opposite direction in the questionnaire shown in Appendix D, with 1, "Very likely," to 5, "Very unlikely." We have reversed the coding here when reporting results for consistency with the reporting of our other results, such that increases in scores are associated with more positive responses.

**Figure 4.4. Likelihood of 17D Participants Staying on Active Duty
Compared to All Air Force Officers**

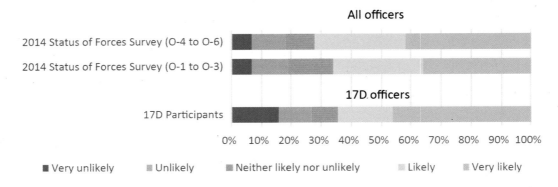

All officers

2014 Status of Forces Survey (O-4 to O-6)

2014 Status of Forces Survey (O-1 to O-3)

17D officers

17D Participants

0% 10% 20% 30% 40% 50% 60% 70% 80% 90% 100%

■ Very unlikely   ▨ Unlikely   ▨ Neither likely nor unlikely   ▨ Likely   ▨ Very likely

The second question was, "How would you rate the overall quality of work done by the 17D community?" The responses to this question ranged from 1 to 5 (1, "Very poor"; 2, "Poor"; 3, "Fair"; 4, "Good"; 5, "Very good").[4] The average response to the question on the quality of the work done by the career field was a 3.3.

Comparison to the 2015 Federal Employee Viewpoint Survey

To help put the views of our 17D participants in context, we also compared our results to the DoD-wide averages reported on similar items in the 2015 Federal Employee Viewpoint Survey. As can be seen in Table 4.3, there are some statistically significant differences (shown in yellow). Most notably, our 17D participants believed the resources available to them were insufficient, the overall quality of work was lower, and that they did not have the appropriate job-relevant knowledge and skills. They also were not willing to say that the 17D workforce was successful at accomplishing its mission. In addition, it is interesting to note that the response to the item about innovation is no different from the response observed on the FEVS. This is surprising given that innovation was one of the areas that cyber personnel in this study discussed as being critical to success in the cyber domain. We also see differences when it comes to liking the work and believing the work is important. In both cases, responses were significantly lower among our 17D participants.

The last question in which we see differences addresses satisfaction with pay and allowances. Notably, in this case, responses from our participants were higher than that of the 2015 FEVS sample. This runs counter to the belief that cyber personnel are dissatisfied with the pay in the military because their civilian options are higher; it is, however, consistent with the statements

---

[4] Note that the item is coded in the opposite direction in the questionnaire shown in Appendix D, with 1, "Very likely," to 5, "Very unlikely." We have reversed the coding here when reporting results for consistency with the reporting of our other results, such that increases in scores are associated with more positive responses.

Table 4.3. 17D Survey Compared to Federal Employee Viewpoint Survey Results

Items posed to 17D career field	Mean	Items posed to FEVS	Mean	p-value
How satisfied are you with pay/allowances?[a]	3.89	Considering everything, how satisfied are you with your pay?	3.43	0.001
How satisfied are you with your current duty assignment?[a]	3.79	Considering everything, how satisfied are you with your job?	3.64	0.177
I like the kind of work I do.	3.79	I like the kind of work I do.	4.13	0.001
The work I do is important.	3.76	The work I do is important.	4.32	0.001
I feel encouraged to come up with new and better ways of doing things.	3.63	I feel encouraged to come up with new and better ways of doing things.	3.53	0.502
I am given a real opportunity to improve my skills in my organization.	3.46	I am given a real opportunity to improve my skills in my organization.	3.57	0.348
My talents are used well in the workplace.	3.34	My talents are used well in the workplace.	3.44	0.331
How would you rate the overall quality of work done by the 17D community?[b]	3.32	How would you rate the overall quality of work done by your work unit?	4.17	0.001
My workload is reasonable.	3.19	My workload is reasonable.	3.39	0.095
In my organization, senior leaders generate high levels of motivation in the workforce.	3.12	In my organization, senior leaders generate high levels of motivation and commitment in the workforce.	3.06	0.617
In my organization, senior leaders generate high levels of commitment in the workforce.	3.09	In my organization, senior leaders generate high levels of motivation and commitment in the workforce.	3.06	0.835
Creativity and innovation are rewarded in the 17D workforce.	2.93	Creativity and innovation are rewarded.	3.05	0.318
The 17D workforce has the job-relevant skills necessary to accomplish the mission.	2.92	The workforce has the job-relevant knowledge and skills necessary to accomplish organizational goals.	3.69	0.001
The 17D workforce is successful at accomplishing its mission.	2.92	My agency is successful at accomplishing its mission.	3.95	0.001
The 17D workforce has the job-relevant knowledge necessary to accomplish the mission.	2.86	The workforce has the job-relevant knowledge and skills necessary to accomplish organizational goals.	3.69	0.001
The 17D community has sufficient resources (budget, equipment, technology, software, etc.) to accomplish the mission.	2.38	I have sufficient resources (for example, people, materials, budget) to get my job done.	3.08	0.001

NOTE: Statistically significant differences relative to FEVS answers are shown in yellow (where the 17D response is lower) and green (where the 17D response is higher). Sample size for the 17D survey is <= 107, and for the FEVS survey <= 73,000. Except where otherwise specified, the response scale ranges from 1, "Strongly disagree," to 5, "Strongly agree."
[a] Scale ranges from 1, "Very dissatisfied," to 5, "Very satisfied."
[b] Scale anchors are 1, "Very poor"; 2, "Poor"; 3, "Fair"; 4, "Good"; 5, "Very good."

made in several discussions suggesting that bonuses are not likely to be the solution. It is important to note that the FEVS includes enlisted individuals in addition to officers, and enlisted personnel have lower pay scales. Consequently, it would not be surprising to find that officers are more satisfied with their pay than enlisted personnel, on average. Consistent with this—as seen on a similar item in the 2014 SOFS—on average, Air Force enlisted satisfaction with pay was only 3.5, whereas officer satisfaction was statistically significantly higher at 4.1.

Significant Differences by Primary Work Type and Grade Group

Respondents self-identified as doing the majority of their work within five types of work: OCO, DCO, DoDIN operations within the 24th or 25th Air Force, DoDIN operations outside the 24th or 25th Air Force, and "Other" (not belonging to any of the aforementioned categories). In total, 94 of our 107 survey respondents self-identified as fitting into one of those five groups.[5] Table 4.4 summarizes the breakdown of our sample based on these work types; "Unspecified" refers to those who did not respond to that item.

Table 4.4. Sample Sizes by Work Group

	OCO	DCO	DoDIN 24th/25th	DoDIN Other	Other	Unspecified
Sample size	24	20	9	12	29	13

We explored whether there was a statistically significant difference in responses across the work types. Such difference was not found when analyzing across work types for questions concerning career intentions, permeable service, interest in a technical track, duty assignment satisfaction, career satisfaction in general, work enjoyment, a decision to stay on active duty, or the quality of the work done by the 17D community. In fact, only across eight variables was there a statistically significant difference in responses depending on work type.[6]

In terms of satisfaction with different aspects of the career field, five variables had a significant relationship with work type. The results of these variables, in terms of their average response across specific work types, ranging from 1, "Very dissatisfied," to 5, "Very satisfied," are presented in Figure 4.5. Most notably, we see significantly more dissatisfaction by the DCO respondents for the items about opportunities to command and lead, unit readiness, and retention of 17Ds, and significantly more satisfaction by the "DoDIN Other" respondents on the quality and content of IQT and IST relative to the responses of the other groups.

Regarding agreement with different aspects of the 17D cyber community, three response variables had statistically significant differences across work type. The responses to these questions, which range from 1, "Strongly disagree," to 5, "Strongly agree," are presented in Figure 4.6. Here we see those personnel self-identifying as "Other" (meaning that their work does not fit well within the groups we listed) as viewing their workload as significantly more

---

[5] The remainder failed to respond to that item.

[6] We set our threshold for statistical significance at $p < .05$.

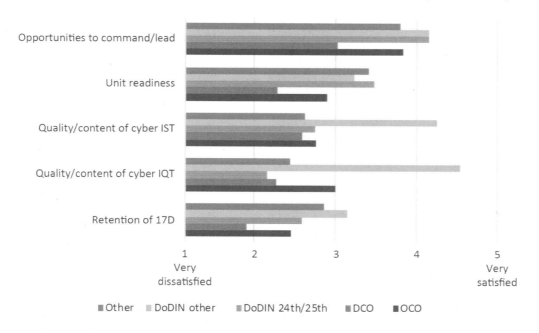

Figure 4.5. Items Showing Statistically Significant Differences by Work Group

Opportunities to command/lead

Unit readiness

Quality/content of cyber IST

Quality/content of cyber IQT

Retention of 17D

1 Very dissatisfied — 2 — 3 — 4 — 5 Very satisfied

■ Other   ■ DoDIN other   ■ DoDIN 24th/25th   ■ DCO   ■ OCO

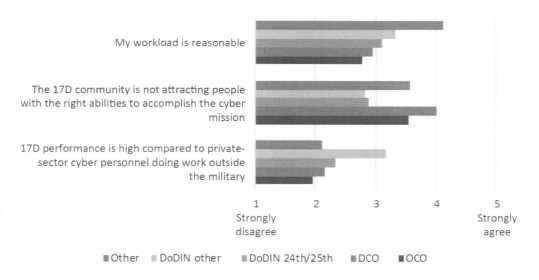

Figure 4.6. Average Agreement with Specific Statements About the 17D Job Across Work Types

My workload is reasonable

The 17D community is not attracting people with the right abilities to accomplish the cyber mission

17D performance is high compared to private-sector cyber personnel doing work outside the military

1 Strongly disagree — 2 — 3 — 4 — 5 Strongly agree

■ Other   ■ DoDIN other   ■ DoDIN 24th/25th   ■ DCO   ■ OCO

reasonable than that of other groups. Although we cannot know what type of work the members of "Other" cyber assignments held, it is likely a mixture of personnel who are serving in special duty assignments, administrative assignments, or other uncommon assignments (e.g., executive assistants, instructor positions, cyber research jobs). Another interesting difference is that our DoDIN respondents were significantly less likely than others to believe that the career field was having trouble attracting people with the right abilities. Lastly, "DoDIN Other" respondents were significantly more likely than others to believe that 17D performance was high.

We also looked for statistically significant differences across two grade groups: FGOs (majors, lieutenant colonels, and colonels) and CGOs (captains and lieutenants), though we found statistically significant differences on only one item: satisfaction with pay/allowances. Majors, lieutenant colonels, and colonels were more satisfied on average with their pay/allowances than were captains and lieutenants ($p <= .003$).

Although we did find statistically significant differences (by grade group and work type) on at least some items, two caveats regarding the statistical significance information reported here are warranted. First, when conducting multiple tests of significance, the likelihood of finding statistical significance by chance alone is increased. For that reason, it is possible that we found a statistically significant difference where none really exists. Second, it is worth noting that because our sample sizes are so small, our power to detect statistical significance is very low. This means that differences would need to be quite large in our data to be detected as statistically significant. It is entirely possible that if this study were replicated on a much larger sample, several other items would show statistically significant differences as well. For both of these reasons, we suggest continuing to explore potential differences (especially by work type) using larger samples.

Open-Ended Comments

Participants also provided detailed written comments on the questionnaire and extended oral comments in our interview discussions. We provide highlights of the findings for both here.

Features Participants Like Most and Least About the Job

Of the 107 survey respondents, 101 provided written responses to the question concerning what they like most about their jobs, and 98 provided responses to the question concerning what they liked least. Figure 4.7 shows the proportion of respondents who mentioned each factor as something they liked most about their job. Figure 4.8 shows the same information about what they liked least.

The responses in these figures were echoed in the focus group discussions.[7] When asked why people join the career field, the most frequently mentioned reasons (discussed in 30 to 60 percent of the discussions) were having an interest in technology, technical problems, computers, or cyber; thinking tech tasks are cool and hacking is great; wanting to serve their

---

[7] For more on how the focus group and interview discussions were analyzed, see the description provided in Chapter Three on the approach to analyzing KSAOs.

Figure 4.7. What 17Ds Like Most About Their Job

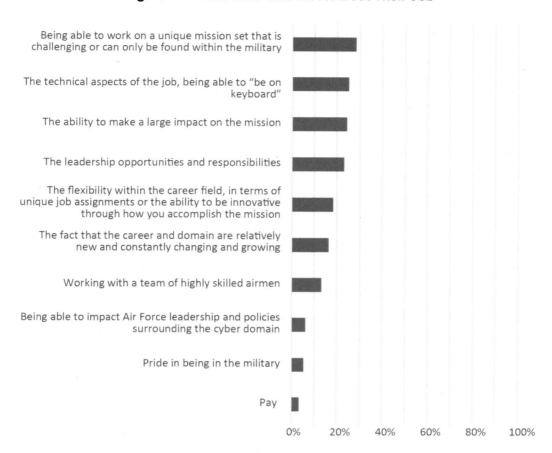

country; prior career field failure or an inability to get their first career field choice; the provision of training and development opportunities; and leveraging their STEM degrees and prior work experience.

Moderately mentioned reasons (mentioned by participants in around 20 percent of the discussions) were the transferability of their cyber skill sets to the civilian sector; the compatibility of cyber with their personality and career goals; helping to grow the 17D career field; the provision of military benefits and advantage of the military lifestyle; their personal prowess regarding technology and computing; the ability for cyber to satisfy a variety of interests; and the confluence of IT and leadership.

Less frequently given reasons (mentioned in about 10 percent of the discussions) included the ability to travel and relocate to different air bases; the provision of leadership opportunities; the influence of family members with a military background; and the challenging nature of cyber-oriented tasks.

Figure 4.8. What 17Ds Like Least About Their Job

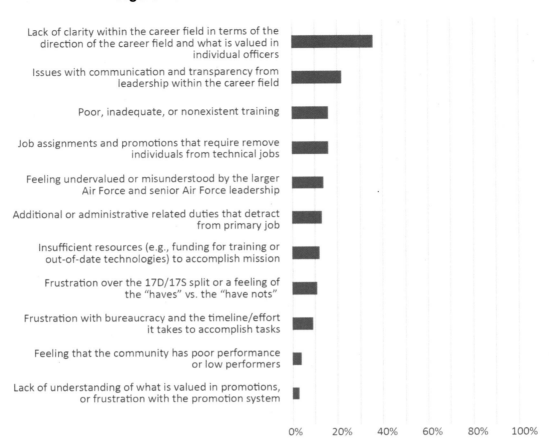

We also asked about why people leave the 17D career field. The most frequently given reasons (mentioned in 50 to 80 percent of the discussions) were low pay and better opportunities in the civilian sector; dissatisfaction with the assignment process; the inability to "stay on keyboard" or "remain technical"; and military culture and career field instability.

Note that the response about personnel leaving due to low pay and better opportunities elsewhere is interesting because, as shown in Figure 4.2, our participants on average indicated they were satisfied with their pay. Nonetheless, these findings may not be in conflict. During our discussion, there were some anecdotes offered about people who had left and obtained high-paying jobs. And this does seem plausible, since it is known that highly competent cybersecurity professionals can command high salaries in the private sector. We also repeatedly heard such statements as, "Why would I stay and put up with [any of the reasons for dissatisfaction] when I can leave, get paid more, and get to stay on keyboard?" However, we also heard from 17Ds who said that those high-paying jobs were not necessarily available to just any 17D. In fact, some acknowledged that they would not be competitive for those jobs themselves, explaining that they did not have the right skill sets or training, would need to amass more years of experience, and so on. In addition, it may be true that many are satisfied with their pay, but the few who are leaving may not be.

Reasons for dissatisfaction that came up to a moderate degree (mentioned in 25 to 40 percent of discussions) included being unsure of one's contribution to the overall mission; lack of resources in the 17D career field; lack of technical expertise and development opportunities; stress (in general); dislike of task-specific policies; better treatment of 17Ss compared to 17Ds; and pressure to assume leadership roles.

Less frequently mentioned examples (mentioned in around 10 to 20 percent of discussions) included dislike of cyber training due to its perceived irrelevance; dissatisfaction with the promotion process; little control over job tasks; and the personal sacrifices that training requires.

Example quotes in response to the first question (what 17Ds like most about their job) are shown in Table 4.5. Example quotes in response to the second question (what 17Ds like least about their job) are shown in Table 4.6.

Table 4.5. Example Quotes: What 17Ds Like Most About Their Job

The possibility of doing unique work in service to the nation that I wouldn't be able to do elsewhere. Additionally, the nature of the work changes from day to day, and significantly changing work roles every few years keeps things interesting. Having the option to extend in jobs I really enjoy, along with the flexibility to move on from ones I don't, is also an upside.

I enjoy seeing the evolution of cyberspace as a tool of military power. I enjoy what we can be versus what we currently are. As a profession, I enjoy getting a breadth of experience in different aspects of the cyber domain. We're at the forefront of a new operational arena. I'm a life-long seeker of wisdom and knowledge. Leading airmen on the frontier of innovating, improving, and defining the capabilities of the future and how we'll operate is humbling. We're still way behind the private sector on many things we do, and we leverage many of their capabilities and tools. But our ability to operate as a national capability is something the private sector can't offer. That is what is great about being a 17D.

As a 17S, what I like most about my career field is the opportunity to use my education and my skills to contribute to the mission. This means I am "on keyboard" doing technical work to solve some of our Nation's tough problems, and receiving validation from having a significant contribution to our National Security.

I truly enjoy being immersed in cyber. I couldn't imagine myself working support, maintenance, medical, or other occupations. I love learning more about what makes computers and networks tick, I enjoy troubleshooting when things go wrong (which they always do), and I love having a sense of service by securing networks, training local defenders, and bettering my skills to defend systems more effectively. I wouldn't trade my field for anything!

My career field is constantly evolving and facing new challenges. There are numerous opportunities to learn and be innovative.

[I appreciate the] [o]pportunity to accomplish the mission while working with phenomenal airmen.

Table 4.6. Example Quotes: What 17Ds Like Least About Their Job

Large percentage of my time wasted on ancillary duties. Looming threat of a non-technical assignment/lack of control over assignment process. Necessity of interacting with undertrained/under-skilled colleagues. Non-competitive compensation compared to private sector.

Bureaucracy. Additional duties that pull away from the mission. Retention. Watching highly skilled/qualified individuals either be force shaped or separating due to the 17D career field mismanaging assignments or not providing a clear vision for career progression/development.

Within the Air Force, the career field management is very poor. Control over assignments by the member is non-existent. Operationally, the ability to control and affect the product the member is tasked with providing is held at the strategic level, leaving the member to handle administrative duties instead of operational priorities. Funding for required training isn't routed to units held to those training standards. Outside the Air Force, there isn't an effective strategic plan for cyberspace. Cyberspace operators aren't utilized according to their ability. Senior DoD and U.S. government leaders repeat the same mistakes of Vietnam. DoD doctrine emphasizes centralized command and decentralized execution, but strategic leaders make tactical cyber decisions.

Without a doubt, the fact that the Air Force does not seem to value cyber one bit . . . we continue to mortgage our Air Force networks . . . we continue to demand more and more of our cyber workforce, and we blame our men and women when systems fail . . . even though we've FAILED to make the NECESSARY investments for DECADES. Cyber has been a pickup game, funded with end of year funds for as long as I can remember. We can spend billions on satellites and aircraft, but a few million to ensure those systems are secure . . . let's leave that to end of year fall out. It's simply insane. You want to know why folks are leaving? It's because they are NOT VALUED. PERIOD.

1. Lack of initial training and programmed skill development. We're not pilots, but consider their regimented and deliberate training paradigm over a career for an example of a better course of action (COA).
2. Functional myopia: I don't think Air Force cyber does a great job of integrating multidisciplinary knowledge/skills. The career field has seemed hyper-focused on maintaining its manning minimums, rather than trying to understand/define exactly WHAT a cyber officer really is.

Haven't used UCT training since UCT. My job is mostly administrative-level busy work. Bureaucracy is too [unintelligible] to accomplish anything. No opportunity to lead. No opportunity to be "on keyboard." Expected to have "warrior ethos," but no chances to do anything warrior-like.

Criticisms of Training

During the discussion, we also asked participants for their thoughts on training, although many raised the issue long before we arrived at that question in our protocol. Taken as a whole, the majority of the comments suggest that training could be improved.

In eight of the discussions, participants offered uniformly positive statements about training. In contrast, in about 75 percent of the discussions, participants raised numerous concerns about training and stressed a need for it to be improved. For example, there were a number of criticisms of the quality of UCT. Participants described such early career training as inadequate, outdated, and in some cases simply incorrect. According to one participant,

> I'd love to say that it's gotten better since I went through. It hasn't, and I went through in 2014. I went through [the] 200 [course] in 2011, and it wasn't very good then either. You go, "Well, what have you done to help fix it?" Well, I gave them an entire page of written feedback, like, single-spaced, saying here's how you can fix it, and from what I can tell, they did nothing with that. I'm not the only one; basically everyone I know that has gone through those courses, that knows anything about that domain, has said, "Yeah, I finally just sat down in the back and stayed quiet, because it hurt a lot less to do that." I have two friends

who went through it the same time, and any time that they said something that was incorrect, or misleading, one would turn around to the one who had already accepted his fate, would turn around and look at the other one who hadn't quite done it, just watch the veins pulse on his forehead. I appreciate what they are trying to do, but at this point, over a half a decade it's been not done correctly. The Air Force, the 8570 system [system of certifications needed for DoD 8570 compliance], is set up for defensive stuff, instead of to help make better system administrators, they're requiring the entire 17D force to do it. I understand the logic, it is a significant burden on the personnel to do it.

Some felt the content was misaligned with the need:

[T]hat would be my biggest complaint coming from the outside, now working on the inside with the Air Force. My biggest complaint would be the actual UCT 17D cybertraining that you get. In my opinion, it's almost irrelevant to what we do. They don't cover things that, in my opinion, pertain to your job. They—it's a lot of head knowledge, kind of learning, and even that is very unhelpful. It doesn't prepare you for the job, so when you get into your actual field, you know the terms, how computer can control an AC unit, but as soon as you start your job, you're thrown into a position where they're asking technical about a laptop computer, and you didn't cover that. I think that can be greatly improved; honestly, I think that they try to cover too broad of a scale.

[S]o those guys need to know how to shoot an exploit using Metasploit at a computer. And then the most frustrating part about that is the base comm guys fill that block and lose sleep at night, and the exploit that they're using is ten years old. So we're testing them on something and creating a significant emotional event on technology that's not relevant anymore anyway

I think right now the length—so, I happen to have someone who's at UCT right now. The length is fine. It's just the—six months is probably about the right length of time for UCT. Reexamining what they're studying and making sure that it's timely is more important. When it comes to warfighting mentality, studying orders that were written four years ago isn't a really good way to go, and that's what's happening right now. They're learning what a cybertasking order is, and they're seeing a version of it from three years ago. As opposed to the one that's current right now. That's not helping them when you're getting on into the career field. They're being taught joint planning by another [lieutenant] who just happened to be there who's never done joint planning before. But he's tasked to do the joint planning block, and he's maybe two years older than them. That's not a good way to get to success or to get to retention.

Some also believed that the focus should differ depending on work type:

I think it needs to be separated into the support piece and the operations piece. Having a general knowledge of what the operator does is great, but again, 80 percent of the 17Ds are providing support functions and are never going to have to program a router. They're never going to have to watch firewalls. Its good knowledge to have, but I think a lot of the training needs to focus on base comms' support.

If 51 percent of the students you're teaching a topic to aren't going to use it, why are you teaching it to them? Right? I don't know where you draw that line.

51

Fifty-one percent seemed pretty low to me, but it seems conservative enough to where I wouldn't get laughed out of the room. If more than half of your students will never use what you're teaching. And part two is if they aren't going to use it for the next eight years, then teach it to them at the year mark, right? So what I would do is build this pipeline that teaches just the basics at the beginning and then à la carte based on unit. Call this the system IUT, right, like you learn the weapon system when you get there or right before you get there, [as] opposed to learning offense even though you're never going to do offense.

I think having the different shreds is okay, but you need more specific training and more diversified options across the board for UCT, it's, yeah, you can test out of blocks and maybe advance through the course further, and maybe at the end of the course you can or maybe you're really . . . or halfway through your— what is it, nine months? Six months? Two point six months. When I went through, it was six [months of] UCT. But I don't know what it is now.

There were, however, those who believed there was value in putting DoDIN personnel through DCO-type training early on in their careers:

Yes, so I would say that there is still a need, even if you were to go to more of the IT side of the house, to understand some of the defensive and offensive—because you can't effectively defend a network if you don't know how it is going to be attacked. I do still believe that is an accurate—but how much of that is on your IT folks versus the folks that are working out of those offices? And, maybe it's not quite as in-depth as it has been, but—it's never not beneficial for them to see that.

It helps a lot. In my one year tour at AFIT [Air Force Institute of Technology], at the company, I was on the defensive side. And, over there, watching sensors, watching our adversaries come in through the company network, that brought me more perspectives on the IT side. To know what we do on securing our side does make a significant difference. We're not just following some checklist provided by DISA [the Defense Information Systems Agency] as a stake, it is because these hardening settings actually stop our adversaries from coming in. Even, yes, an exchange with the other side helps. It just depends where that exchange may be.

Many participants also talked about how this early training experience set people up for disappointment. They talked about how training in everything up front can be wasteful because it atrophies over time when not used, and the technology changes too quickly anyway. For example:

I spent my last two years doing training, so I have strong opinions about how the training is structured and could be structured better, and we're working on it. I think the training for the officers is too long now for everybody. It's too technical and creates the impression that everyone is going to be doing these highly technical things for their career, and it creates disappointment when they get to their first units and they're not doing that. I think that there should be a baseline. This is what you need to know to be a cyber guy if they go to a cyber hands-on job, then they go to a the requisite training because those skills are perishable, so if we train you as a [second lieutenant] and then send you to two assignments where you work in a comm squadron, then we want you to do cyberops, you'll have forgotten everything you learned and it's going to be difficult to relearn it in advanced training . . . when you go to one of those missions you have to go . . . and get another month or so of specific training for that. That bubble, that sphere. When you move from one series to another as part of your PCS [permanent change of station], you go back for training for what you're about to do . . . that would be a fundamental restructuring of how we do the training, but we can still keep the career field merged, where we can go back to ACT to get skills topped up and go to IQT for [the] weapons system, then go out to the mission, and if you're leaving that area to go back to base comm, there ought to be something for that. Like, "Here's what changed that last three years since you did base comm," because it changes fast.

Some talked about the need to focus more on developing leadership, officer skills, and communication skills. Many also talked at length about the need for more warfighting skills, strategic and operational thinking, a bigger-picture understanding of the military and the role of cyber within it, and the need to start developing early in an officer's career. For example:

Maybe in UCT we need to spend a month not learning OCO, but spend a month learning what the AOC [Air Operations Center] does in an air war fight. Because, we're not teaching that.

How would I do, well, as far growing people from a leadership perspective? I think the Air Force starts too late in teaching people about the military decisionmaking process, about deliberate training, training in general, because most of the 17 guys, they don't touch it until they're majors. The Army? They start it before they are even lieutenants, and they just pound it into them from day one. It makes them much better as far as making decisions, it makes them better at analyzing options, both tactically and operationally, and also strategically. The Air Force, however, does a fantastic job hemming and hawing and building decision matrices, and color briefs, and stuff like that. It does not lead to being decisive under a time crunch.

I believe those are important so we understand military and not just 17; we need to understand the different career fields, what they do and how they do it, and to also do joint planning and joint doctrine as well.

JP 5 [Joint Publication 5], that whole military planning process. We're coming to it as Air Force officers at this rank, which is way too late.

I'm lucky I had [a] plans job in '08 where I did cyberplanning as a captain transitioning to major. Even then it was too late. What we need to do is get them to understand, if they're going to be in an operational job, they have to understand the difference between tactical, operational, strategic-level plans and why the Air Force and military does what it does out of COCOM [combatant command]. And it shouldn't be an alien language to us when we walk into a COCOM, or advise a commander when he's talking about the different phases of war, when he's planning out his missions—where should you pipe in for planning—

Lastly, some talked about the need for more resources for training, including the need for simulators, ability to attend in-residence training, better manning to allow people to attend training, and the cost associated with purchasing commercially available training. For example:

The money isn't there to buy the training because a lot of our training is commercially produced. The money isn't there to buy the training, and the manning isn't there to allow me to step away from my desk to go get that training.

I don't want to leave it too gray, or be too politically correct in my answer, but I'll say, and it can be based on sometimes the unit you're in and what that mission is, and how the importance of that mission is seen by higher-level entities. I've seen times, being involved in cyber for just a few short years now, where it seems like the flow of resources have been dried up to a desert, and I've seen resources at times flowing down like a monsoon, and it seems largely driven by the climate or what's going on in the country. Even the civilian leadership at the congressional levels, and the higher levels of DoD. Sometimes we are reactionary, sometimes we can be kind of kneejerk depending on what happens. If you look back to the OPM [Office of Personnel Management] hack, I mean, cyberentities and defense, you could get all you wanted. But if a new threat emerges, if a new focus comes up as far as our government is concerned, you may see resources shift, that well dry up a little bit. I see that our training that I see our men and women getting at this level is excellent. I mean, root9B, Mandiant, FireEye, some of the training courses that our folks are going is being taught by civilians, so they're getting the same thing that industry gets. The conferences, DEF CON that people go to, it brings in professionals across the industry from worldwide. So, our folks have those opportunities to engage and receive that same training that the folks in the private industry get, but it can come in different pulses of surge and then drawing back, so it's not always that constant flow, and I don't think it will be that until we as a nation to keep this streamlined, and we're not frustrating folks with, okay, now we're doing this, okay, now we have to shift our focus. Because that's just the climate of our nation. We know as a military service that sometimes things are driven by what the demand is. Sometimes our leaders overcommit, sometimes they undercommit, but they do what they can, conduct the analysis that they can to best direct resources at a certain snapshot in time.

Additional Comments

Following extended discussion about the reasons people stay or leave, we asked participants if there they were satisfied with the direction in which the career field was headed and, if not, what else could be improved. In response, they raised a number of additional concerns about the way the field is managed and resourced, its culture, and leadership's vision for the future.[8]

Frequent comments (mentioned in between 50 and 90 percent of the discussions) included the perceived need for high-level leadership in the cyber enterprise to communicate vision, foster creativity, improve leadership treatment of cyber, increase face-to-face contact, and help increase

---

[8] It is important to note that this information was not provided in direct response to the question about what leads personnel to stay or leave the career field. Nevertheless, to the extent that these topics are leading to dissatisfaction within the career field, they could impact recruiting and retention in the long term. In addition, even if they do not impact retention or recruiting, many people expressed concerns that they may be leading to tangible effects on their ability to do their job, the quality and cost of the services they are providing the Air Force, the ability of the Air Force to defend against potential cyberattacks, and overall mission success.

knowledge in the field and the existence of leaders with cyber knowledge; that career pathways were not clear enough or too dissimilar from other career fields; that more resources were needed or other concerns about weapon systems; concerns about the identity crisis associated with including 17D versus 17S or DoDIN versus OCO and DCO jobs and lack of vision for the career field; dislike of assignments and job rotations; dissatisfaction with promotions, performance evaluations, performance feedback, and opportunities to recognize and manage high performers; the benefits of having a separate competitive category for cyber.

More specifically, at the top of the list of concerns were issues that had also been described by some of our SME participants. For example, concerns were expressed about how leadership views cyber, including the fact that many leaders do not fully understand the risks (or lack of risks) inherent in various cyber activities, leading them to make decisions that members of the cyber community feel are misguided. Many also discussed the need for a clearer organizational structure of leadership for the cyber community, raising concerns about the fact that there are potentially multiple owners of the cyber domain, none of whom seem to serve the best interest of the enterprise (AFSPC has primary oversight, SAF/CIO manages the career field, joint commanders place demands on the career field, etc.). Some noted that a move to ACC might lead to improvements, though they cautioned that that too seemed not to be an obvious fit. Some even noted that it might make most sense for cyber to be an entirely separate service.

Along similar lines, participants noted that the Air Force has made cyber one of its core missions. Yet participants felt that actions were speaking louder than words—that is, the resources and management of the field suggested to them that Air Force leadership had yet to fully embrace that mission, or perhaps still did not fully understand how best to support the mission. That manifested itself in concerns about the fact that leadership has not provided a clear vision for the community. Participants felt it was critical for them to better understand how their work (both on the DoDIN side and the offensive/defensive side) impacted the Air Force's mission. In their view, that vision should be communicated and understood at all ranks, and the links between the strategic vision for the force and the vision at the operational and tactical levels need to be made explicit for the community.

Participants also had opportunities to provide additional comments in their survey responses. Seventy respondents provided comments for the question, "Is there anything else important about the 17D job or quality of life that we should know about?" Forty-three provided comments in response to a prompt at the end of the survey, "Please provide any additional comments here." Seventy-six individuals offered comments in either one or the other area. Because both of these response options were so open-ended, we have selected quotes that highlight themes seen throughout the survey and offer particularly detailed recommendations. Example quotes in response to the first question (the 17D job or quality of life) are shown in Table 4.7. Example quotes provided at the end of the survey (additional comments) are shown in Table 4.8. Again, many of the sentiments are similar to those expressed during the focus group discussion.

Table 4.7. Example Quotes: Additional Information About the Job or Quality of Life

We've spent a lot of time and effort training new LTs to be cyber operators, but most of them will go to comm squadrons where they're in a support role. As mentioned above, it's important for them to have a thorough understanding of the domain, but I think we're painting a false picture in initial skills training of the sort of thing they'll be doing in the Air Force, so that when they get to their unit they're disappointed and starting out at a morale deficit. We're unintentionally making "support" and "maintenance" dirty words by calling everything "operations," and the true operational community sees that a huge portion of what we do is support or maintenance, and our marketing campaign costs us credibility. Sometimes it is a cyber operation—reserve that word for those cases. Build understanding and appreciation for how critical cyber support and maintenance are for EVERY other mission area.

There is still lack of understanding at Air Force senior leadership levels in that cyberspace operations = maintaining the network, i.e., email.

The reason you will get a wide swath of answers is because the career field is too broad and the senior leaders, for reasons I'm not sure of, seem to like it that way. We were very close a few years ago to doing what we needed which was bifurcating the 17 community into two AFSCs (cyber-warfare, cyber-ops), but it became apparent that young officers wanted cyber-warfare and were not excited about the 17D core communications mission. That prompted a re-merger which was wrong! We needed specialization and we can't get there trying to do IT, IT security, and OCO all in the same AFSC family.

Stress is high and conflicts w/ family life.

Senior leaders right now are busy trying to figure out the overall direction of cyber right now and we have a major void in top down communication. Guidance and the direction of the career field is extremely difficult to find. Where there are a number of middle-management FGOs who give their two cents on this base on what they have seen and heard, I don't feel adequate downstream info is available. I also think we are pushing a false narrative to many of our younger 17Ds/enlisted as far as what they are signing up for. We talk cyber hunter/kill missions and high-end net defense, then turn around and send them to run the ADPE [Automated Data Processing Equipment] account at Malmstrom AFB [Air Force Base]. Those jobs need to be done, but we need to find the carrot for the end of that tour.

My opinion is that you would get better career satisfaction with better expectation management at the beginning. For example, if new Lieutenants understand from the beginning that they would become leaders of help desks, network operations, client support, server admins, C2 systems, COMSEC, post office, and deployable comms. Don't put kids in UCT with the hopes that only a few will make it into the cyber operations career field. ALL graduates of UCT should go directly into operating cyber weapon systems. Establish a separate course for kids who want to go into comm support roles. Just my background, I spent two years working in the industry as a programmer, before graduating from OTS [Officer Training School] to become an officer programmer. I then attended [undergraduate training in another Air Force high-demand career field], and became a [member of that other career field] for [several] years, before moving back into comms.

Lots of lip service about how important cyber is with no funding year after year to get after systemic issues plaguing of domain. The ORB [officer retention bonus] is a start, get why would I stay if they're letting the building burn down around me and blaming me for it? Zero investment in the enterprise outside "we found money" speaks louder than the retention bonus.

I'd like to see more flexibility to cross-flow in/out of cyber. I understand there is a compelling manning crisis, but the white-knuckle death-grip that Air Force cyber holds over its personnel creates the impression that I'm simply a warm body and +1 on the metrics slide. I'm functionally stove-piped to study "cyber-things" in post-grad programs or career-field sponsored training rather than dare look outside the box of cyber to explore alternative thoughts/methods to solving difficult strategic problems. If my educational background in business, foreign language, and behavioral science weren't factors that prevented my selection to and continuation in the 17D field, why aren't they supported/endorsed now? Intel, pilots, personnel, security forces can all explore other disciplines. Why can't/shouldn't cyber?

Definitely enforce a sense of value and belonging for both 17Ds and 17Ss. There's an invisible rift between the two. Make sure each feels they can succeed. One is more support oriented, leading hundreds and having wide influence. The other is more operational with little to no leadership but gets the cool missions. We're compared to each other for promotions, so ensure both feel valuable.

Bonuses are/were a step in the right direction. Stop sending people with no cyber knowledge/skills/education into the career. Warrant officer construct has great value for cyber. Cyber needs its own MAJCOM [major command] and/or component command. More IT training is needed. We don't have the people or money to succeed at cyber as a service.

Air Force senior leaders definitely like cyber and want to support it. The problem is [that] intent and vision aren't manifesting into reality. Slowly change is occurring. Our training is not molded with a vision of where we are ultimately going. We're always building the airplane as we fly it. Certain cyber jobs in the Air Force are amazing. Others are dreaded. It creates a lot of stress on our officers going through the pipeline. Every job in the cyber field should be coveted and sought after, regardless of location. Pilots going through UPT [Undergraduate Pilot Training], may not always get to fly the latest fighter jet. It's competitive, however, at the end of the day, all 17Ds should be executing cyber operations, whether on the offensive line or defending a weapon system. Not supporting and maintaining.

Table 4.8. Example Quotes: Additional Comments

We enforce cyber too broadly. At the same time, our leadership pyramid is too small. We must broaden our defined leadership roles, so people receive commensurate recognition. Alternatively, we must define our different mission sets and focus heavily on a technical track. Moreover, redefine our career development. Allow members to interview and compete for senior leadership roles when they want. Don't force progression, but use feedback to evaluate. In addition, offer greater access to transition between civilian and military service, via Reserves. Increase duty location durations to allow for greater specialization. Our cyber forces are heavily centralized. Separate away the "comm" roles.

The six-month cyber tech school vastly under prepares its officers for working in the field.

Money is only half the battle. We're currently being used as bodies to click buttons rather than brains to innovate and engineer solutions.

I think you'll find similar issues between cyber operators and pilots. There are plenty of jobs on the outside offering more money than the military will ever be able to match. However, money is not what will keep individuals here. Rather, the ability to innovate and fully use their cyber skills will. Let people train, learn, develop, test, and execute in operational environments. Give them a faster more agile acquisition department to get new tools and software and an accreditation process to get it on the network rapidly. Lastly though, don't tell them that they'll be going back to a paper pushing job when you've awakened their creative and technical energy. That is a morale killer, and you will see people leave to go do cyber elsewhere.

I can't stop emphasizing how bad the training is: (1) UCT schoolhouse is a mess. I was personally told by the schoolhouse to create courseware only weeks after graduation on a subject matter that I had no background or training in . . . if that gives you any indication as to the rigor of the course. The curriculum was fumbled together by random officers (versus experts in the subject matter) assigned to the schoolhouse and it was clearly a rush job if you interview graduates. The joint course equivalent (Joint Cyber Analysis Course), in comparison, has its own oversight committee (w/ reps from each branch) that has to collectively agree to changes to the curriculum that has a proven track record for rigor throughout the joint community. (2) CWO [chief warrant officer] [course] redundantly instructs material already taught in UCT (which points to a disconnect between the two units). It spends very little time on topics/concepts that require lots of effort to learn and critically think about to fully grasp (programming is one to two weeks . . . not nearly substantial enough). Its tests require little thinking (just regurgitate concepts or examples shown during class) and the quality of its graduates reflect that. (3) The Initial Qualification Training for some of the DCO units doesn't address nearly enough to transition a person to the duties required of them at each of the units. One of the reasons is that the Master Training Task List (MTTL) doesn't accurately represent the training tasks for each weapons system . . . the MTTL defines what tasks a weapons system operator needs to be trained to and at what level. The MTTL also directly shapes the written and performance evaluations that, if a person passes, signify that the operator is "Mission Ready" or fully trained to do their job. Our communities can't agree to a comprehensive MTTL so everything tied to it falls apart. Our "Mission Ready" is a misnomer. (4) The Air Force HAS TO transition to joint equivalent training. The MAJCOM MUST take ownership/leadership of the training it signs off on (but the community creates on its own with no oversight) we can truly identify the respective community's training needs.

I believe there needs to be a fundamental change on how we focus cyber and comm. The two worlds are different and require different training and expertise. Treating all comm as cyber pushes support comm to the background as the cyber gets all the funding/manpower and publicity. Having equal support for cyber ops and support level comm is important.

I believe our primary problem is poor organization of forces due to failure to properly analyze and decompose strategic objectives. This creates (1) tactical unit confusion and scoping difficulties, (2) equipping ineffectiveness as the PMO take on too many ambiguous requirements, and (3) training ambiguity and breadth of surface knowledge versus effective tactical skills. These feed off each other, poor tactical tasks creating more training ambiguity and requirements ambiguity, weapon systems scope creep increases training ambiguity and perceived tactical "capability." Training ambiguity creates individuals lost, directing more ambiguity. The operational level restates strategic concepts as training, passing an idea like "mission assurance" down to the tactical level to solve. AO thrashing based on opinions and subtle employment method idea differences stalls tactical strategic consensus and development of standard operational ideas is stalled by too many chefs working on the same problem, creating factions and divisions. Decisions made are used as leverage to enforce agendas, and endless posturing wears me out.

I've watched problems identified by tactical units be filtered by the operational level, all with good intentions, preventing simple strategic decisions from being made, or from being made with a complete as possible picture of the problem. Combine this with low pay and great external opportunities, why would anyone want to stay? Our effectiveness is low, our policies restrictive, we are overly tasked with SQ additional duties, told to spend but can't buy what we really need, and can see others (contractors) doing our job better

Air Force cyber will fail if we do not allow technical experts to focus on their specialty. I'm not a technical expert but it's painful to watch the technical geniuses I went through UCT with leave, not because they are not being paid enough but because they are being forced to focus on EPRs [Enlisted Performance Reports], etc., when their passion is cyber. It's not about the money. Hopefully they'll tell you that when you survey them . . . they tell me all the time. Cynicism hurts retention. Cynicism in this career field starts at IST. This occurs because a large number of students have a significant emotional experience trying to pass OCO and DCO blocks of instruction on information they will not use. If >51 percent of 17D CGOs do not use it, why is it in the CFETP [Career Field Education and Training Plan]? Fix the CFETP, shorten IST and extend follow-on billet-specific training. Very small portions of the career field use the information gleaned from UCT blocks on Integrated Air Defense, Space Systems, Telephony or Industrial Control Systems but that takes up a month of training. Use the IQTs that already exist to teach this information right before an officer goes to a billet where they need it. The hacker methodology and anatomy of an attack is great background info and it would be ideal if all 17Ds had this knowledge, but trying to shoe horn 100 percent of the career field into understanding OCO may not be the right answer. Again, the CFETP should represent those skills that are common for > 51 percent of the career field. Not enough skills are common for that much of the career field? Then the definition of the career field is too broad and we need to split it in to pieces! The vector letters for the 2010 and 2011 year groups from last year's fall DT had a tremendously positive influence. I know several officers that got notified they were in the bottom third, that had skills to do better but had never received honest feedback and did not know where they fell. These officers are already on a better path.

Suggestions for Changes to Help Recruiting and Retention

Lastly, we asked participants to identify initiatives or changes that could be made that would help retention or attraction of high-quality personnel. Their responses included a range of suggestions, with many repeated across a large portion (around 40 to 50 percent) of the groups.

The first was that many people felt that the 17D workforce was not being well served by grouping members of the DCO and OCO community with the DoDIN operations personnel. This concern manifested itself in the training discussion presented previously, but it also came up in the context of promotions, personnel wanting to stay technical, the fact that movement of personnel from one type of cyber work to another leads to costly training, downtime while people get up to speed, and a lack of depth of understanding of any area.

Some suggested that a technical track would be a good solution for keeping people who are interested in staying "on keyboard" and honing their craft. A warrant officer track was another option that was cited for the same reason. Some felt that allowing personnel to stay technical for longer would not only benefit retention but also would lead to a more technically competent force for executing missions. It also was cited as an opportunity to develop what some called "technical leaders." These were not leaders in the traditional Air Force sense (developed to lead in any capacity), but rather individuals who would be well suited to overseeing and managing high-functioning technical teams that specialize in one area within the cyber workforce (i.e., specialized to lead personnel in one or more areas within DoDIN, OCO, or DCO operations).

Many noted that turning some of the DoDIN support and maintenance responsibilities over to civilians or contractors could help reduce the demands placed on the 17D community, reduce the disappointment many see in being placed in DoDIN assignments, and possibly even improve support and maintenance services for the Air Force. However, they also acknowledged that doing so may be costly for the Air Force, may be hindered by red tape, bureaucracy, overly restrictive contracting rules, and other similar constraints. They also noted that even if the Air Force did shift that work away from being a core 17D function, the shift would take many years to fully execute. A few raised the possibility of increased vulnerability and security concerns if the work was outsourced, and a few noted that it might reduce the Air Force's understanding of potential threats to network security if it did not have core military personnel who were well-versed in the support functions.

Another frequently mentioned topic was increased agility for the acquisitions process, citing that the process was entirely unfit for changes that need to occur at the speed of cyber. This however was universally viewed as an immovable issue, and one that was often discussed alongside concerns that the Air Force simply is not structured in a way that allows for the flexibility that is ideal for cutting-edge cyber operations, or for being proactive (as opposed to reactive) in cyber support and maintenance.

For all of these ideas (e.g., civilians, warrant officers, technical tracks, and splitting the career field) there were opposing points of view; however, in all cases the number opposing an idea was outweighed by the number of discussions where comments were offered in support of it.

Summary of Key Findings and a Note about Their Interpretation

Our discussions with SMEs and members of the 17D workforce yielded a number of interesting findings about sources of satisfaction and dissatisfaction within the career field, many of which they also speculated were drivers of attraction and retention. The following are areas they discussed frequently:

- Many want to be able to do technical work for longer in their career.
- A perceived lack of clarity in the vision for the cyber workforce is hindering the mission and morale. Little connection is made between strategic vision and tactical task on which the workforce focuses on a day-to-day basis.
- Assignments to 17S are typically viewed as more attractive, but few such assignments are available, leading to widespread disappointment.
- Retention of personnel with 17S experience may be a concern, especially if they fear being shifted away from 17S assignments when their service commitment is up.

- There is a perceived mismatch between the training provided and the skill levels of people completing it, the type of work people will be doing (information network support versus offensive cyber operations versus defensive cyber operations), and the practical day-to-day procedural information needed in the field.
- Critical technical acumen may be atrophying as a result of not allowing cyberspace professionals to stay in technical roles or providing adequate continuation training during their careers.
- Some do not feel as though the cyber mission is adequately resourced; this includes resourcing manning, training, simulators, and cybertechnology.
- The Air Force's acquisition and decisionmaking processes are not agile enough to address the cyber enterprise's needs.

That said, a note of caution in interpreting these findings is warranted. Although these were themes that were mentioned as sources of dissatisfaction within the community by numerous groups and individuals, it is important to remember that the results presented in this chapter only give us insights into people's perceptions on these issues. Those perceptions may or may not be grounded in reality; for example, it is possible that the Air Force's acquisition process is very agile, flexible, and responsive to the cyber community's needs, despite a perception that exists to the contrary. For that reason, more research may be needed to explore the facts behind the community's views on some of these issues, and to the extent that leadership questions whether certain beliefs are based in fact (whether training is poor, acquisition lacks needed agility, resources are inadequate, etc.), additional research testing out the premises behind those concerns ought to be pursued.

Nevertheless, these are the views held by the people we talked with, regardless of whether those views are based in fact. It is therefore also important to point out that the existence of a shared negative perception or shared concerns in a workforce ought not to be ignored for two reasons: First, it may signal that in fact there may be truth in the perception (perhaps agility in the acquisition process is a real problem), and second, perceptions matter because they influence people's behavior. That is, if personnel perceive a problem (even it no such problem exists), it can still lead to dissatisfaction and other negative outcomes, including attrition. For that reason, taking action to either fix the problem or change the perception that there is a problem is a critical step in combating any problems with retention or interest in the career field.

5. Conclusions and Recommendations

In this study, we reviewed existing research on cyber workforce KSAOs, analyzed personnel data files to further explore the retention problem within the 17D community, and met with a range of SMEs and members of the workforce to get their views on critical KSAOs, as well as major sources of dissatisfaction and drivers of attraction to and retention in the career field. Taken as a whole, these research efforts suggest that cyber leadership should consider making a number of changes to how the cyber enterprise and the career field are managing to address these concerns, which we discuss in the remainder of this chapter.

Before discussing those recommended changes, however, is important to point out that the changes we suggest below are based entirely on people's perceptions of the problems within the community. In the absence of any evidence to suggest otherwise, we are assuming that the perceptions offered by our participants reflect real issues in the community, but we acknowledge that perceptions are not always correct. This is an important caveat to the recommendations provided below, and one that should be explored further by leadership before implementing any recommendation, if it believes that perceptions related to these recommendations may not reflect reality. Regardless of whether there is truth in these perceptions, as noted in Chapter Four, perceptions do matter because they influence people's behavior. If in fact people's perceptions are reflecting a misperception rather than a true problem, leadership should still seek to address the problem, but the approach should be different. In that case, leadership should take steps to address any misperceptions and should follow up later to confirm whether perceptions have changed as a result of leadership's attempts to address it.

That said, and assuming that the perceived issues reported by our participants are real, we offer the following changes for leadership to consider.

Consider Formally Managing the Cyberspace Operations Officer 17D and 17S Positions as Distinct Career Fields

A broad array of comments offered by our participants were fundamentally related to the tension between the functionally different jobs that exist within the 17D community. The research literature suggests that maintaining a single career field for all cyber domain functions potentially has negative consequences.

The negative consequences of maintaining a single cyber career field emerged in themes related to multiple phases of the career life cycle. Recruits who are specifically interested in DCO and OCO are potentially deterred from entering the career field because of the possibility of spending a significant amount of their careers doing traditional IT (Yannakogeorgos and Geis, 2016). Interview participants indicated that sending all 17Ds through a common operations-focused training pipeline both underprepares DoDIN operators and potentially harms their morale by creating a disconnect between expectations and reality. Cyber personnel are treated differently across the functions, which has created questions over the types of career development experiences that future promotion boards will value most (leadership experience versus operational impact). Finally, maintaining a single career field will likely result in DCO and OCO operators being involuntarily cycled through DoDIN assignments, which prior research and interview participants' responses indicate will decrease their job satisfaction and retention.

One possible way to alleviate some of these struggles is to formally manage 17D and 17S operators as distinct career fields, analogous to the different pilot career fields (fighter pilot versus mobility pilot). Still, there are several arguments for maintaining a single, yet more operational, cyber career field. First, the career field is in transition, and the balance of DoDIN versus DCO and OCO is in flux, while the DoD role in IT provision is expected to decrease. With a common career field, it could be considerably easier to manage these fluctuations. There could also be value in exposing officers to both types of missions. Finally, the number of 17S positions is small, and a formal division of the functions could unintentionally bar 17S personnel from opportunities and reduce their visibility and influence, especially at the higher grades.

On the other hand, there are potential benefits to splitting apart the career field, and doing so does not necessarily mean that efficiencies of having a single career field would have to be lost. For example, separating the career fields would not preclude having core training that is common to both, nor would it mean that there could not be significant interaction across the career fields as the functional roles change over time. The 11X pilot specialties are distinct career fields,[1] yet they share a common undergraduate training pipeline and interaction across fields plays a strong role in manning certain communities (in the special operations and reconnaissance fields). Further, despite the expected decrease in traditional IT, 17D personnel will likely maintain some role in DoDIN operations going forward. And finally, there is support in corporate practice for organizing and managing IT and information security as distinct functions (Schmidt et al., 2015).

That said, policymakers will ultimately need to weigh the costs and benefits of a career field split in making a decision about whether such a split would be advisable. In order to weigh the costs and benefits, the Air Force would need to first carefully think through and specify the details of several reasonable alternative course of actions (COAs) for how the two career fields could be managed. Examples of the some of the details that should be specified and considered and that might differ meaningfully across a range of COAs include:

- numbers of personnel expected at all grade levels
- types of assignments or billets that would need to be filled at all grades

---

[1] Pilots are assigned to a specific airframe for the entirely of their flying career. They cannot switch aircraft without retraining.

- number of accessions needed
- whether the command structure that exists now for overseeing personnel would need to change
- expected career development paths
- planned numbers of personnel interaction across the career fields (as occurs in pilot career fields)
- management of training entirely distinct training tracks or some combination of common and distinct
- a distinct vision for the strategic, operational, and tactical roles for the members of each career field and its place within the Air Force's overall mission (which might differ by COA)
- changes to who is attracted to and accessed into each career field (differences in requirements, characteristics, etc.) and how many are successful in training and on the job.

And some examples of the consequences that should be explored for each COA include:

- whether the number of billets at each grade would be in line with the expected number of personnel in the career field at those grades
- whether the planned career paths provide sufficient development of personnel to be competitive for leadership positions at the colonel and general officer levels
- anticipated impacts on perceptions by personnel inside and outside the career fields, and how they might affect satisfaction, retention, and recruiting within the career field
- anticipated impacts on delivery of services and on meeting mission (changes in resources for cyber work, visibility, leadership support for the work, leadership's understanding of its value or how it can be leveraged, etc.)
- anticipated impacts on personnel management costs, workload, manpower allocations, and operations tempo
- expected retention rates within each community and anticipated impacts on retention going forward
- anticipated impacts on promotion rates for each career field
- expected impacts on the ability of the career fields to advocate for resources, reach leadership as needed, etc.
- unintended consequences.

SMEs and stakeholders in the cyber workforce, as well as others experienced in management of in-demand career fields (those involved in rated personnel management), would likely be good sources of ideas for a range of ideal COAs and the potential consequences of each. Establishing a working group of those stakeholders and SMEs to flesh these out could be a first step toward further exploring this path.

It is also worth noting that there are a number of lessons to be gained from the way that the pilot force has been managed over the years that could help inform any decisions on how to manage the 17D/17S workforce going forward. For example, the shifting culture of the 17D force from a *mission support* mentality to an *operator* orientation may be part of what accounts for the perceived "tribalism" within the cyber workforce. As the cyber workforce grows, that tribalism may become more entrenched, not unlike what has been witnessed in the rated force. That is, mobility pilots, fighter pilots, bomber pilots, helicopter pilots, and CSOs maintain separate cultures with an internal "tribal" friction. One factor contributing to this tribalism is how pilots have been selected for certain pilot tracks in the past, a process that shares some similarities with how 17Ds have been selected for 17S assignments. For example, prior to the introduction of Specialized Undergraduate Pilot Training, some graduates used to be classified as qualified for Fighter Attack or Reconnaissance. Those not classified as such were required to go to "heavies" (a specific type of aircraft), primarily in the mobility air forces. This created an early, pre-UPT graduation schism that brought the perception of a first-class and second-class citizenry along tribal lines. Classification for 17D and 17S in UCT seems to have followed a similar path.

Lastly, regardless of whether 17D and 17S should be managed as separate career fields, it may be worth further exploring differences in the training requirements needed in 17D and 17S assignments. A look at the 2017 *Air Force Officer Classification Directory* (*AFOCD*) requirements suggest that the current knowledge and skills needed in 17D and 17S assignments are essentially identical. However, given the discussion by participants suggesting that the two types of assignments can involve meaningfully different types of work, a study examining whether *AFOCD* skill requirements need to be modified to reflect true differences between 17D and 17S requirements may be worthwhile.

Create Opportunities for Cyber Officers to Pursue Technical Depth

A related theme that emerged in both the research literature and interviews is the strong desire of personnel working in cyber to pursue and maintain technical depth. Prior work highlights that technical depth is important to both IT and cybersecurity, and that corporate practices cultivate depth among managers and specialists. Other research also highlights that the civilian sector views career development and training opportunities as key retention tools. In conversations with SMEs, references to strong desires to remain "on keyboard" as long as possible were pervasive, as were fears among members of the cyber workforce of being pulled away from technical duties and relegated to administrative or leadership duties. This theme suggests that technical depth is uniquely important in the cyber workforce and that operational proficiency should be a priority amid other career development goals. Discussions included a wide range of options for allowing cyber personnel to remain technical over the course of their careers (e.g., one SME suggested pilots as a model for balancing depth and breadth). Though the views of participant's in this study did not provide a definitive recommendation on the optimal way forward for fostering this depth, it seems sensible that career field management could at a minimum allow for the development of technical depth in the same way that it does among aircrew personnel.[2]

That said, we note again that this recommendation is based entirely on perceptions by participants that developing technical depth is important for ensuring cyber mission success and that an opportunity to stay technical is desired by many cyber officers. With respect to perceptions that staying technical for longer is desired by at least a subset of the people in the cyber officer workforce, that view appears to be widely held among our participants and our SMEs and not likely up for dispute. On the other hand, with respect to perceived importance for cyber mission success, further exploration of whether this is really true may be warranted, and it can be best answered by conducting a range of additional studies. For example, one approach to exploring this further would be to correlate a range of measures of cyber officer effectiveness (including subjective measures such as supervisory ratings, ratings by commanders) with measures of their technical expertise. Another would be to conduct a task analysis of the officer job to determine which aspects, if any, require technical expertise, as well as the relative importance of those tasks. A third would be to identify the types of critical decisions that cyber officers face in their day-to-day work and conduct an experiment simulating those decisions that is designed to test the quality of the critical thinking and the decisionmaking results of officers with varying levels of technical expertise.

These are just a few examples of research that could be pursued to help inform management of this career field. Collection of additional data and exploration of additional analyses is discussed further in its own section below.

Continue to Prioritize Technical Backgrounds in Accessions, with Pathways for Candidates to Demonstrate Potential in Other Ways

Because cybersecurity is an emergent field, the research literature indicates that there is no single background that is best for cyber operations (though education institutions continue to develop new programs aiming to address this shortfall). Prior research suggests that technical backgrounds should be preferred, but organizations should also look for cyber talent lurking in populations without computer science or engineering degrees. Thus, one strategy is to pursue technical backgrounds while also supporting opportunities for candidates to demonstrate cyber potential in other ways, such as cyber competitions. Recruiting candidates with cyber potential could prove difficult under current labor market conditions, so policymakers should evaluate whether additional recruiting resources are necessary to bring in candidates with the right skill mix. The interview data suggest that undergraduate training requirements differ for those who

---

[2] Note that allowing a commissioned officer to be a career-long technician could run contrary to the expectations for roles and responsibilities of officers in Title 10 of the U.S. Code unless adjustments were made for cyber operator to be viewed as a "profession," as is the current case with military lawyers, doctors, and scientists.

already possess technical credentials, so successful recruiting could enable cost savings through training pipeline adjustments. Thus, taking a *recruit for aptitude, educate for knowledge, and then train for skills* approach for this career field might be particularly beneficial. Lastly, it is worth noting that current Air Force guidance states that only 10 percent of the accessions should be sourced from nontechnical academic degree backgrounds. As such, there may be a need for Air Force manpower planners to reassess current Classification of Instructional Programs (CIP) guidance as highlighted in the 2017 *AFOCD* (Air Force Personnel Center, 2017, Appendix A, pp. 247–248).[3]

That said, this is another instance where perceptions by participants may run counter to what would actually turn out to be best for the career field. As discussed in the prior section, additional research exploring the impact of different types of educational backgrounds on cyber officer performance should be explored. The example studies described in the previous section are also applicable here.

Closely Monitor Retention and Be Prepared to Use the Full Spectrum of Retention Tools

Civilian demand for cyber expertise is strong, which has created broad concern over whether the Air Force will be able to retain sufficient numbers of skilled cyber personnel. The research literature and interview participants point to retention drivers in the areas of compensation, quality of life, and training and career development opportunities. Prior work has shown that many of these factors are linked to retention, but that retention can be manageable despite strong civilian demand for marketable skills provided by the military. Thus, it would be wise to closely monitor 17D subgroup retention patterns (those with 17S experience versus those without it) and address the drivers of low retention as much as possible.

For example, both prior research and our interview participants note that there is currently no additional Active Duty Service Commitment associated with advanced cyber training, but Active Duty Service Commitments are a crucial tool in rated management to ensure a minimum return on training investments. Salaries in information security are rising, so career field managers should monitor compensation differentials and utilize bonuses or continuation pay if necessary to maintain parity. Prior research and our interviews suggested that job satisfaction, even more than compensation, could play a strong role in decisions to remain in the Air Force. Our interviews also suggested that access to state-of-the-art training and technologies could entice people to stay longer (this is also discussed in the next section). If possible under career field management

---

[3] For more on the current academic requirements in officer accessions into the 17D and 17S career fields, see U.S. Air Force (2017).

constraints, policymakers should explore ways to avoid a range of other separation "triggers," such as involuntary reassignments that conflict with individual goals and desires.

In addition, our examination of retention rates for personnel with 17S experience suggests that these personnel are leaving at a higher rate than are others in the career field, again raising concerns that the Air Force is losing vital cyber talent. While retention of those with 17S experience can currently be easily tracked in the Air Force's personnel data files, exploration of retention within more specific 17D subgroups is not so easily explored. For example, there is no designator in the personnel files that identifies whether a 17S assignment is OCO or DCO, and there is no designator for whether a DoDIN position involves base support or some other kind of DoDIN activity. Tracking retention separately within these subgroups may provide further insights into retention. However, such designators would need to be merged with or added to the personnel data files going forward. Lastly, attrition for these subgroups should also be tracked and monitored within the other cyber workforces. Attrition in the civilian and enlisted workforces and in the Air Force Reserve and Air National Guard workforces within these groups is likely to provide useful additional insights that would not only be beneficial for those cyber groups themselves but could also help tease apart issues that are unique to officers versus those that could benefit from policies that take a total force perspective.

Lastly, there is also still a need to assess the impact of the new Blended Retirement program on 17D officer retention. This too could pose additional burdens on 17D retention as many more may now consider leaving before the 20-year point.

Ensure Sufficient Agility in Training, Tactics, and Acquisition

A salient theme in our interview responses was that the Air Force is not postured to keep pace with the rapidly evolving nature of the cyber domain. Our SMEs indicated that the undergraduate training processes for developing and updating curriculum do not move fast enough, and that the content needs to be more adaptable to different student backgrounds. Further, they highlighted a need for more robust and constantly evolving continuation training than is standard in other operational communities. Members of the 17D workforce also offered a number of criticisms of training overall, and argued that the training needs to be ongoing, up to date, and tailored to individual and assignment-specific needs. In addition, many noted that some state-of-the-art training is available, but due to resource constraints only a small, select number of personnel have access to it. Responses also indicated that bureaucratic acquisition processes are not responsive enough, and that such processes limit the ability of personnel to employ helpful technologies, putting them at an operational disadvantage. In general, many SMEs described the Air Force as rigid and risk averse in ways that do not accord with success in the cyber domain. Lastly, other concerns included an expectation of accountability without the localized authority to make decisions, thus causing an inability on the part of personnel to be responsive to the commanders they support.

That said, once again, we note that this recommendation is based entirely on the perceptions of the participants; we cannot know for certain whether there really is a lack of agility in any of these areas. Follow-on research, including collecting perceptions of the agility and responsiveness of cyber personnel to commanders' requests and to mission demands placed on them, would help determine whether this truly is a concern.

Teach Such Concepts as Warfighting, the Mission, Strategic Thinking, and Operational Planning at All Levels

Participants repeatedly pointed to warfighting and understanding the mission set as areas of expertise that define a high-quality 17D but noted that these areas are woefully underdeveloped within the force. They believed strongly that people need a much richer understanding of these topics in general, and the Air Force needs to begin instilling them at much earlier points in airmen's careers (starting as early as UCT). This was viewed as critical for helping to develop future Air Force leaders, improving decisions made at all levels, improving the ability to communicate with leadership and members of the joint community, prioritizing resources, making recommendations, and better serving the needs of commanders. It is worth noting that these are among the types of skills and competencies that have been identified as being relevant for of all Air Force officers (see the Air Force's institutional competency list in U.S. Air Force, 2015). The results here further reinforce that those competencies are germane to the cyber officer job as well, and suggest that more attention may need to be paid to developing them in the cyber officer workforce.

Establish and Communicate a Strategic Vision for the Career Field and Link It to the Tactical-Level Work

Many of our participants noted that there seems to be a large disconnect between the work taking place at the tactical level and the strategic cyber mission that leadership is articulating. These types of comments came from personnel involved in a wide range of cyber activities, including DoDIN base support. This issue was discussed in the context of improving morale and the need for people to understand how their tasks have meaning and impact for the Air Force mission. On the DoDIN side, for example, leadership needs to recognize and provide feedback to personnel on how maintenance and support activities are helping in the fight. Lack of strategic vision also hurts the cyber workforce in other ways. For example, some note that failing to identify the link between senior leader strategic vision for the force and work being done at the tactical level has meant that some work is extremely inefficient and wasteful in a resource-constrained environment: personnel may be focused on tactical issues that may not be relevant in the bigger picture. If the connection were made, leaders could better prioritize efforts and redirect personnel to focus on the most relevant activities. A clear articulation of these links could also help the cyber workforce restructure the entire enterprise to better serve the needs of the Air Force.

Who is responsible for linking the vision at the top to the work at the bottom? Many respondents have suggested that the onus is on midlevel leaders (majors and lieutenant colonels) to establish and articulate that operational-level link for the force. At the time of our research, participants felt that such a link was almost entirely absent from leadership at that middle level. This suggests there may be a need for more development for midlevel leaders focused on articulating and executing the strategic vision at the operational level. It also suggests that the culture and norms for the role of midlevel cyber leadership and for how cyber personnel are led at that level needs to shift.

Our participants also noted that there is a diffusion of responsibility and conflicts regarding who is in charge at the highest levels of cyber leadership, which is hindering their ability to establish such an operational-level link. First, AFSPC had ownership over cyber, although many believe that cyber does not align well with AFSPC's other missions and, consequently, has not received the resources and attention it needs. A move to ACC is in the works, but that too is viewed as potentially fraught with the same challenges. Second, participants explained that because AFSPC, SAF/CIO A6, and the Deputy Chief of Staff for Manpower, Personnel and Services (AF/A1) all have responsibility for managing the cyber workforce, no single individual has been adequately empowered to articulate and execute a career field vision. Most participants believe it falls to SAF/CIO A6 to take responsibility, but they recognize that AFSPC (and soon possibly ACC) would need to be on board to execute it. This has led some to suggest that until a central unifying cyber authority is established (an Air Force Cyber Command is an example), no one will be able to step up and articulate a singular vision in a way that will successfully permeate the enterprise at all levels.

Establish a Forum Through Which to Collect Innovative Ideas for Managing the Cyber Career Field

Officers in the 17D career field may have a number of innovative ideas for managing the field in a way that could improve recruiting and retention. In a few instances, our participants brainstormed some interesting ideas for new ways of doing business that could potentially help address various concerns within the workforce. In those cases, participants also cautioned that idea had just occurred to them, so they had not spent time thinking it through to see if it would work. As a result, more thinking along these lines would be needed. Nevertheless, the following is an example of one creative idea that a member of the cyber workforce offered up.

In the context of addressing concerns about an OCO operator being placed in a DoDIN assignment, one OCO participant explained that he and his coworkers were at the top of their class, and all were extremely technically competent and unbelievably smart. He found working as a team with people at that level to be part of what was so rewarding about the OCO work. He said he would be happy to do DoDIN base support work if he could execute the work in a similar environment. That is, if his high-functioning team was asked to go solve complex DoDIN problems at a base—keeping the members together as a team and giving them a challenging mission—then he would be perfectly happy to stay in the Air Force and do that type of work. And he noted that creating such high-functioning execution teams might be an efficient and successful way to address key aspects of the DoDIN mission. But the prospect of going to a base to work with personnel who did not have the same level of experience and expertise, and being tasked with responding to random service tickets, was not appealing. His coworkers in the room agreed.

Currently there is no system in place for personnel to brainstorm ideas such as this for how to revolutionize the way cyber does business. Establishing such a forum could be an effective way of gathering innovative ideas to improve job satisfaction among cyber operators.

Establish Enterprise-Wide and Forward-Thinking Approaches

Participants pointed to sources of inefficiencies that are causing increased workloads and general frustration within the cyber community. For example, the existence of outdated legacy systems and the fact that some organizations refuse to update or adopt common technology were two complaints. Officers explained that if technology were kept up to date at a pace that mirrored that of the private sector, and if the technology was consistent across the enterprise, it would meaningfully reduce the cyber maintenance and support workload. Instead, training personnel to support multiple platforms or outdated platforms adds burdens on the force.

For the Air Force to be a formidable cyber force against its adversaries, officers believe that it is critical to place a high priority on investments in cutting-edge technology, training, and approaches to doing business. Doing so, however, would require the Air Force to foster an environment that embraces new technologies and cutting-edge concepts. This lack of forward thinking and the failure to move toward enterprise-wide solutions to problems may be resulting in poor support and maintenance on the DoDIN side and potential vulnerabilities and missed opportunities on the DCO and OCO sides. Multiple participants also lamented the fact that they do not have access to simulators that would allow them to test out new ideas and new platforms or practice defending against adversaries.

Explore Recruiting and Retention Challenges in the Air Force Enlisted and Civilian Cyber Communities

The focus of this research effort is on the 17D community. However, going into this study, our sponsor, Maj Gen Patrick C. Higby, also expressed a strong interest in the enlisted and civilian workforce communities. During our discussions with our 17D SMEs and with members of the 17D workforce, participants echoed Major Gen Higby's concerns; they mentioned that the enlisted and civilian workforces may also face challenges in attracting and retaining personnel and suggested that work addressing these communities is also needed. For example, one SME said that replicating this study with Air Force civilian cyber personnel would be of great value, since he was having extremely high levels of turnover within his civilian force. Others described problems in finding and attracting qualified personnel, citing times when civilians who were hired turned out to be incapable of performing the work required. With respect to enlisted personnel, one concern is that the differential between enlisted pay and compensation in the civilian market may be a strong incentive for people to leave. However, some of those private-sector jobs may require college degrees. Given that military enlistments do not, enlisted personnel may not be as competitive in that market. That said, it is likely that many private-sector organizations will make an exception for the best and the brightest. In addition, it is not uncommon for enlisted personnel to possess a college degree or even advanced degrees. As a result, this is another group that could be facing a retention problem, at least among its most skilled personnel. This study, exploring issues among 17Ds, was therefore just the first step to understanding these issues as a whole, and more work needs to be done.

Additional Caveats to Our Recommendations

The goal of this study is to explore attitudes relating to and perceptions about major drivers of retention in the cyber officer workforce. The study is designed to be exploratory, meaning that we held open-ended discussions in which we asked participants to tell us their own top concerns. This has two main benefits. First, it does not presume that we know in advance what those concerns will be. As such, participants are not primed by the researchers to focus on a particular topic. Second, it allows us the opportunity to fully explore what participants mean when they express a concern by asking for examples, probing for more information, and asking follow-on questions.

There are also limitations to the approach, however. For example, one limitation to this type of study design is that it does not typically have as large a sample as might occur on a larger-scale survey because of time and resource constraints; this limits the power of the study to detect significant differences between groups. Another potential downside is that participation may not necessarily be representative of all members of the community, since not all locations can be visited in person (a survey can more easily sample participants from all locations, although not all surveys do). Although those are potential limitations of this type of design, we took steps to combat such issues in this study by holding discussions at all the bases where there were large groups of cyber officers, by including bases that had personnel focused on different aspects of cyber work, by including SMEs representing all aspects of the cyber workforce (including individuals who were working overseas, or in unique but relevant assignments, such as White House communications), and by including not only bases from a range of regions across the continental United States but also Hawaii, which conducts work for the Pacific Air Forces.

An additional concern commonly raised about participation in focus groups such as these is that participants may somehow be different from those who do not volunteer to be part of such discussions. Notably, it could be possible that people who are particularly unhappy are the ones who volunteer, whereas those who are happy do not. Two points regarding this are worth making. First, we asked participants to tell us what they liked about their jobs, in part to determine whether they were truly disgruntled. If they were, we would expect that they would have a harder time coming up with positive things to say. In fact, we did hear numerous positive responses from our participants, with some describing plenty of reasons why they would like to stay in addition to offering thoughtful insights into reasons why they or others might be driven to leave. In addition, the survey results suggest that many of our participants are satisfied with their careers. This suggests that our sample of volunteers did not comprise mostly complainers. Second, even if we did end up with people who were more dissatisfied than the others within the career field, it may not be problematic for the goal of this particular study. That is, if the goal is to identify ideas for how to keep more personnel, talking only with the people who are dissatisfied might provide a number of useful insights.

As noted previously, it is important to point out that this study was designed to describe the workforce's perceptions and views regarding the drivers of retention and recruiting within the cyber community. These views and perceptions are an excellent initial source for recommending initiatives that could improve retention and recruiting, but we cannot know from these perceptions alone whether such initiatives will be successful and, if so, how successful. It is also not known whether any of the perceptions identified here represent misperceptions and those misperceptions themselves are all that need to be addressed. As a result, additional research should be undertaken to explore any areas where leadership believes the prevailing perception is simply a misperception. In addition, for those areas where the perception is believed to be based in fact, research should be undertaken to measure the impacts on recruiting, retention, and satisfaction within the community that result from the Air Force adopting any of the recommendations we offer herein. The results of that research should inform further changes to any initiatives to address retention and recruiting going forward.

Looking Ahead

To lead in cyber, the Air Force needs to be proactive, not reactive. Competition with the private sector for top talent will only increase as demands for cyberspace professionals rise nationally. Thus, it is not prudent for the Air Force to wait for a problem to arise or to worsen before acting. Cyber is a fast-moving field, and its evolving nature affects the interests of the professionals working within it.

The insights gained through this study point to areas where initial steps can be taken to increase job satisfaction, improve retention, and reshape how the Air Force markets its cyber job opportunities to the public. Improving training content and opportunities throughout the careers of cyber personnel is an example of the type of action that could have significant payoff given the importance that cyberspace professionals place on staying current in their field. Ensuring that cyber personnel can remain focused on operational duties for longer in their careers without fear of being transferred to administrative or leadership positions (where technical skill atrophy is likely to occur) is another example.

But this study has only scratched the surface of the range of issues that could be explored to help manage this increasingly vital career field. More research could certainly be done. For example, many of the potential initiatives discussed by our participants (staying technical for longer, or offering technical tracks) have precedent in other career fields (such as the rated pilot force) or other services (such as warrant officers).[4] Further exploration of culture, a training pipeline, skills sustainment, force management initiatives, and lessons learned in other career fields and in the other services could provide additional important insights into these areas.[5]

Other research may also help round out some of the perspectives offered here, including examinations of the issues from a total force perspective to better understand how the Air Force may be able to best leverage the strengths of the Air Reserve, the Air National Guard, and the enlisted, civilian, and contractor components. In addition, lateral views of the practices of other services in managing their own cyber workforces may provide additional valuable insights.

Lastly, being responsive to the workforce should be viewed as a continuous process. It should include additional tracking and analysis of performance, demographics, and other data as described in the recommendations above. It should also include taking steps to determine whether the perceptions by the force described here are signaling that a problem does exist, or whether the views are mistaken and simply in need of correcting through a widespread communication campaign. And, most important, it should include taking the pulse of the workforce at regular intervals to make sure that any steps taken to address the areas of dissatisfaction identified here are having the desired results and that the Air Force is ultimately better able to recruit and retain the high-quality talent essential for mission success.

---

[4] Commissioned officers are expected to lead and progress along specific vertical promotion opportunities; however, exceptions are granted to members of the pilot community.

[5] A review of academic literature behind managing the endless (yet cyclical) pilot retention issue or other high-demand jobs might provide additional insight into cyber retention options. Military health care professionals, scientists, and lawyers are examples of other highly technical career fields that might provide insights into other ways that the cyber workforce could be managed.

Appendix A. Official Descriptions of the 17D and 17S Air Force Specialty Codes

What follows are the complete descriptions of the 17D and 17S designators provided in the October 2017 *Air Force Officer Classification Directory*.

17D CYBERSPACE OPERATIONS
(Changed 31 Oct 17)

1. Specialty Summary. Operates cyberspace weapons systems, employs cyberspace capabilities, and commands crews to accomplish cyberspace, training, and other missions.

2. Duties and Responsibilities:

2.1. Plans and prepares for mission. Reviews mission tasking, intelligence, terrain and weather information. Supervises mission planning, preparation and crew briefing/debriefing. Ensures equipment and crew are mission ready prior to execution/deployment. 2.2. Operates weapons system(s) and commands crew. Performs, supervises, or directs weapons system employment and associated crew activities.

2.3. Conducts or supervises training of crewmembers. Ensures operational readiness of crew by conducting or supervising mission specific training.

2.4. Translates operational requirements into architectural and technical solutions. Works with commanders to deliver complete capabilities that include technical and procedural components. Researches or oversees research of technologies and advises commanders on associated risks and mitigation factors in conjunction with meeting requirements.

2.5. Directs extension, employment, reconfiguration, adaptation and creation of portions of cyberspace to assure mission success for combatant commanders. This includes both deliberate and crisis action scenarios.

2.6. Develops plans and policies, monitors operations, and advises commanders. Assists commanders and performs staff functions related to this specialty.

3. Specialty Qualifications:

3.1. Knowledge. Knowledge is mandatory including electronics theory, information technology, telecommunications and supervisory and control systems including cryptography, vulnerability assessment and exploitation techniques. Additionally knowledge will include operational planning, governing cyberspace operations directives, procedures and tactics.

3.2. Education. For entry education requirements see Appendix A, 17D CIP EducationMatrix. 3.2.1. Prior service 1B4 or 1N4X1A commissioning Airmen will be accepted into the career field regardless of undergraduate degree possessed.

3.3. Training. The following training is mandatory as indicated: 3.3.1. For award of AFSC 17D2X, completion of Undergraduate Cyberspace Training (UCT) and mission qualification training in suffix specific area.

3.4. Experience. For upgrade to AFSCs 17D2X/3X, unit commander determines proficiency based on performance, experience and completion of minimum training requirements.

3.5. For award and retention of 17DX, specialty requires routine access to Top Secret or similar environment and completion of a current Single Scoped Background Investigation (SSBI) according to AFI 31-501, *Personnel Security Program Management.*

NOTE: Award of the entry level without a completed SSBI is authorized provided an interim Top Secret clearance has been granted according to AFI 31-501.

4. *Specialty Shredouts:* Suffix

Suffix	Portion of AFS to Which Related
A	CDA—Cyberspace Defense Analysis
B	CSCS—Cyber Security and Control System
C	AFINC—Air Force Intranet Control
D	CVA/Hunt—Cyberspace Vulnerability Assessment/Hunter
E	C3MS—Cyber Command and Control Mission System
F	ACD—Air Force Cyberspace Defense
Y	General
Z	Other

17S CYBERWARFARE OPERATIONS
(Changed 31 Oct 16)

1. Specialty Summary. Operates cyberspace weapons systems and commands crews to accomplish cyberspace, training, and other missions.

2. Duties and Responsibilities:

2.1. Plans and prepares for mission. Reviews mission tasking and intelligence information. Supervises mission planning, preparation and crew briefing/debriefing. Ensures equipment and crew are mission ready prior to execution/deployment.

2.2. Operates weapons system(s) and commands crew. Performs, supervises, or directs weapons system employment and associated crew activities.

2.3. Conducts or supervises training of crewmembers. Ensures operational readiness of crew by conducting or supervising mission specific training.

2.4. Develops plans and policies, monitors operations, and advises commanders. Assists commanders and performs staff functions related to this specialty.

3. Specialty Qualifications:

3.1. Knowledge. Knowledge is mandatory including electronics theory, information technology, telecommunications and supervisory and control systems including cryptography, vulnerability assessment and exploitation techniques. Additionally knowledge will include operational planning, governing cyberspace operations directives, procedures and tactics.

3.2. Education. For entry education requirements see Appendix A, 17S CIP EducationMatrix. 3.2.1. Prior service 1B4 or 1N4X1A commissioning Airmen will be accepted into the career field regardless of undergraduate degree possessed.

3.3. Training. The following training is mandatory as indicated: 3.3.1. For award of AFSC 17S2X, completion of Undergraduate Cyberspace Training (UCT) and mission qualification training in the suffix specific area.

3.4. Experience. For upgrade to AFSCs 17S2X/3X, unit commander determines proficiency based on performance, experience and completion of minimum training requirements.

3.5. Other. 3.5.1. For award and retention of these AFSCs, specialty requires routine access to Top Secret or similar environment and completion of a current Single Scoped Background Investigation (SSBI) according to AFI 31-501, *Personnel Security Program Management.*

NOTE: Award of the entry level without a completed SSBI is authorized provided an interim Top Secret clearance has been granted according to AFI 31-501.

4. Specialty Shredouts: *Suffix*

Suffix	Portion of AFS to Which Related
A	CDA—Cyberspace Defense Analysis
B	CSCS—Cyber Security and Control System
C	AFINC—Air Force Intranet Control
D	CVA/Hunt—Cyberspace Vulnerability Assessment/Hunter
E	C3MS—Cyber Command and Control Mission System
F	ACD—Air Force Cyberspace Defense
G	NAS—Network Attack System
J	Offensive Cyberspace Platforms

Appendix B. Insights from the Existing Literature on Recruiting and Retaining a Competent Cyber Workforce

Given the picture of the broad requirements for cyber operators described in Chapter Three, the task of career field planners is to determine a strategy for which characteristics should be part of recruiting (i.e., screening), and which should be trained or developed.[1] Further, such a strategy also needs to retain sufficient numbers of operators with the right skills to sustain the career field. The following sections discuss the implications of the existing research for Air Force planners regarding recruiting and retention. These sections will focus on the implications for the 17D workforce, but the reader should recognize that there are also challenges and potential opportunities in the enlisted, civilian, and contractor segments of the Air Force cyber mission.

Recruiting Officers with Cyber Potential

A key question in recruiting cyber operators is to determine which KSAOs (if any) should be prerequisites for entry into the career field. Plainly, should the Air Force seek to buy or make cyberspace expertise? The existing research on the labor market for cybersecurity expertise suggests that attempting to attract proven cybersecurity talent would be exceedingly difficult, as there is currently strong competition for cybersecurity workers. Raytheon (2014) released a report describing demand for cybersecurity personnel as rising 3.5 times higher than other IT professions and 12 times higher than the overall job market. Further, while other occupations have drawn on increases in the female labor supply to meet demand, women account for less than 10 to 15 percent of cybersecurity job roles (LeClair, Shih, and Abraham, 2014). Studies have noted that this high demand is likely to bid up wages for cybersecurity workers, especially those at the high end of the talent spectrum, and that government salary constraints could be a barrier to recruiting (Libicki, Senty, and Pollack, 2014; Vogel, 2016; Westermeyer, 2008).

One advantage that the Air Force has over civilian companies is that it can offer access to exciting areas exclusive to national security, such as offensive cyber operations. However, even in this area, the Air Force must compete with other national security and government agencies, and recent data suggest that the Air Force is behind other federal entities. For example, among recent graduates of the Scholarship for Service program (the largest government-funded cybersecurity scholarship program), only a small fraction went to work for the Air Force, while a

---

[1] Note that officer training and development in the Air Force already advocates development of competence in leading airmen, as well as other associated institutional competencies, extending beyond the tactical level, through the operational level, and into the strategic level as someone progresses in his or her career. For more information, see U.S. Air Force (2017).

third of all graduates ended up at the National Security Agency (in part due to its reputation for hiring the best hackers). For this reason, the DoD *Cyberspace Workforce Strategy* (*CWS*) lists partnering with other agencies to establish a national cyberspace talent pipeline among its strategic focus areas (U.S. Department of Defense, 2013).

These limitations indicate that the main way Air Force planners will recruit people who already have some cyber expertise is through targeted accessions in assigning new officers to the 17D career field. The *CWS* endorses this idea, calling for DoD agencies to "leverage ROTC [Reserve Officers' Training Corps] programs and the service academies to inject more cyberspace elements, seek more cyber-related majors, and, where applicable, place them in cyberspace jobs once commissioned" (U.S. Department of Defense, 2013). Yannakogeorgos and Geis (2016) recommend that ROTC budgets be increased to recruit 17D officers with the right education backgrounds using targeted scholarships. Jabbour (2010) recommends an education including mathematics, computer science, computer engineering, electrical engineering, and physics to provide the academic foundation for a career in cybersecurity, which are all areas listed among the Tier 1 fields of study for 17D in the 2016 *AFOCD*. Yannakogeorgos and Geis (2016) emphasize the particular need for computer and electrical engineering backgrounds, because computer science curricula do not focus on the unique characteristics of cyberphysical systems (embedded processors in weapon platforms). Further, focusing on particular education backgrounds could bear more fruit in the long term as cybersecurity education programs expand. Yet, in the short term, there is an imperfect relationship between degree field and cybersecurity talent (Libicki, Senty, and Pollack, 2014), which means that the best strategy also likely involves attempting to attract those with the right aptitude and developing them into top-tier cyber operators.

In the absence of widely recognizable indicators of cyber talent, organizations have used different methods to identify interested individuals with potential. Some organizations have used outreach events and contests ("hackathons") to identify raw talent.[2] The use of screening tests for cyber potential has been discussed in past research, but not in the context of officers. The Air Force has a long history of aptitude screening for its pilot career fields (Carretta, 2011) and has developed and implemented cyber aptitude screening for enlisted operators (Trippe et al., 2014; Yannakogeorgos and Geis, 2016). There is also a joint effort under way to develop a test that screens specifically for OCO and DCO aptitude that could potentially be incorporated into the Air Force Officer Qualifying Test (the written test that is currently used in pilot screening). Further, Campbell, O'Rourke, and Bunting (2015) have proposed a framework for developing screening tests for cyber aptitude, as well as a prototype test known as the Cyber Aptitude and Talent Assessment. Currently the career field relies on demonstrated aptitude during UCT to

---

[2] The Air Force Association's CyberPatriot contest is one example, though it is not meant to be an Air Force recruiting tool. Yannakogeorgos and Geis (2016) describe CyberPatriot as a "starting point," but the authors question the wisdom of the defensive-only focus of the contest.

determine officers who are tracked for DCO and OCO (versus DoDIN operations). At this early stage, no validation information exists on the effectiveness of the current approaches compared to other potential screening strategies, but this is certainly an area that merits further study.

Finally, the service academies are a useful tool to steer high-aptitude officer trainees toward cyber and help them build knowledge and skills. Service academies offer the opportunity for curriculum that is tailored to military applications; both the U.S. Air Force Academy (USAFA) and the U.S. Naval Academy have recently created undergraduate majors in topics related to cybersecurity and cyber operations). Because they are not responsible for operational missions, service academies also have a sort of research and development capacity to test new concepts, such as the CyberWorx program that debuted at USAFA in 2017 (Moix, 2017). For these reasons, USAFA may be uniquely suited to identify and develop the small number of high-capability hackers that the Air Force would have difficulty recruiting otherwise.[3]

Retaining Skilled Cyber Workforce Professionals

In seeking to develop a skilled cadre of cyber personnel to perform its missions, the Air Force faces a predicament. The military, civil service, and commercial spheres are all extremely reliant on networks for conducting business, and all parties realize that those networks are vulnerable to costly attacks. These twin forces—the ubiquity of networks and the rapid realization of the cost of vulnerability—have created a bidding war for the limited pool of cyber workforce professionals. Further, public-sector entities (such as DoD) have considerably less flexibility in wages and benefits, which puts them at a disadvantage in attracting and retaining top talent. Thus, several high-profile reports point out that shortages are worse for the federal sector and that these shortages create significant national security risk. (For a survey of the market for cyber workforce professionals in general, see Libicki, Senty, and Pollack, 2014.)

It is also worth noting that for private-sector organizations, shortages are less of a threat than they are for the military, as lateral entry is both possible and commonplace. Losses of personnel at any experience level can be mitigated by simply hiring personnel to replace them. In contrast, the long-term health of any career field in the Air Force depends on whether it can retain the right personnel with the right experience levels in sufficient numbers.[4]

---

[3] One potential drawback to attempting to develop cyber talent among USAFA cadets is that relatively few have significant operational knowledge and experience on which to draw. Attempting to build an understanding of engineering robust networks without an understanding of how those networks are integrated into operations could be "putting the cart before the horse." Yannakogeorgos and Geis have found that USAFA cadet perceptions of 17D work could also be a barrier to drawing high-aptitude officers into the cyber workforce. Their interviews with cadets and faculty elicited that cadets are reluctant to choose the 17D career field because they fear getting "'stuck' serving as a base communications squadron officer instead of doing 17-series work" (2016, p. 158).

[4] While it is possible that lateral entry of personnel could be allowed at some point in the future, it runs counter to the Air Force's goals of developing officers with years of experience in the organization to serve in leadership roles.

The booming labor market for cybersecurity talent presents a headwind that Air Force planners must manage over time, but the fact that cyber operators have marketable skills does not preclude the maintenance of a healthy 17D career field. In discussing retention in the emerging cybersecurity field, past research focuses on three main dimensions: compensation, quality of life, and career development. Though there continue to be many challenges in maintaining sufficient numbers of rated operators, a bulwark of rated management has been the combination of retention bonuses and service commitments, which planners can calibrate continuously based on civilian labor market conditions (Mattock and Arkes, 2007; Mattock et al., 2016).

Compensation for cybersecurity personnel is rising (Suby, 2015), but the DoD *CWS* shows that senior leaders recognize the need to use traditional force management tools to retain cyber specialists. Further, the high levels of compensation commanded by elite professionals in the civilian labor market does not necessarily pose a problem for the career field as a whole. Schmidt et al. (2015) present evidence that pay and benefits for military personnel are competitive with salaries among corporate IT and cybersecurity personnel, and they highlight the idea of targeted retention efforts for personnel with uniquely valuable skills. However, Wenger, O'Connell, and Lytell (2017) explain that actual postservice earnings might differ from that of the perceptions of military members, so expected earnings could play a role in retention even if there is relative parity in compensation levels between the military and civilian sectors. In sum, most sources agree that labor market conditions call for proactive monitoring and the use of traditional retention tools in managing cyber career fields.

The discussion on the retention impact of nonmonetary, quality-of-life factors has acknowledged potential problems in several Air Force communities, including pilots (U.S. House of Representatives, 2017), remotely piloted aircraft operators (Hardison et al., 2017), and intelligence personnel (Langley, 2012). Recent Air Force research indicates that active duty cyberwarfare operators are also at increased risk of occupational stress compared to civilian operators (Chappelle et al., 2013). Furthermore, a recent survey of corporate practices in managing cyber workforces notes that job satisfaction, rather than high salaries, is the focus of retention efforts in the private sector. The authors of that study list "good working environments, belief in the mission, opportunities for training, exposure to and engagement with professional organizations, and access to interesting assignments" as factors contributing to job satisfaction (Schmidt et al., 2015). A key takeaway for the 17D career field is that persistent differences between Air Force and civilian quality of life could lead to elevated attrition.

A related area that is often mentioned in cyber research involves career development—specifically, how technical skill is managed and fostered.[5] In the *2015 (ISC)² Global Information Security Workforce Study* (Suby, 2015), training initiatives ranked highest in importance to

---

[5] Technical skills could be managed in similar ways to gaining and maintaining private-sector certifications, such as those offered by a host of private firms. See https://cybersecurityportal.com/resources/certifications/ and https://certification.comptia.org/certifications/cybersecurity-analyst for additional info.

retention—higher, even, than compensation. Hosek et al. (2004) have concluded that the value of training and career growth in the military was instrumental in retaining adequate numbers of IT workers during an analogous labor market boom in the late 1990s.

While the DoD *CWS* stresses that "DoD must expand educational and training opportunities" and "career progression needs to be flexible, with a rich diversity of job and career opportunities" (U.S. Department of Defense, 2013), there could be retention-harming disparities in this area between DoD and civilian employment. Corporate practice stresses cultivating technical skill among leaders, which makes them better managers, and adjusting the work employees do to keep them interested (Schmidt et al., 2015). Yet, the drive in the officer promotion system to become generalists could be at odds with developing skill depth in the cyber field, and the Air Force assignment processes continually face a trade-off between individual desires and filling critical positions (Yannakogeorgos and Geis, 2016).

Concluding Thoughts

Improving the nation's cybersecurity has received a great deal of policy emphasis and study in the wake of several high-profile and costly attacks. Yet, the KSAOs that professionals need in order to improve cyberspace operations are not so well defined that wide standardization and formal academic training can meet demands. Qualities like technical acumen, critical thinking, and leadership and communication skills are recognized in the literature and by cyberspace experts and members of the cyber workforce in the Air Force. Within the Air Force, the importance of a "warfighting mind-set" and operational understanding is also highly important. But there is less agreement on the type of education needed, and the need for STEM degrees versus a variety of other academic backgrounds.

This puts the 17D career field in a position where it must chart its own course to providing cyber capabilities (in conjunction with national security partners) by attracting raw talent and continually investing in job satisfaction and skill development. Yet the 17D career field need not work in isolation in determining its appropriate path, as there are lessons to be learned from parallel paths such as the rated pilot career path in force management principles. It is clear that long-term mission success requires no less than successful recruiting, development, and retention of officers with many of those same traits. However, given that research also suggests that the Air Force will face challenges recruiting and retaining that cyber talent, a focus on ensuring job satisfaction and quality of life, adequate compensation, and professional development in keeping with that found in the private sector will be needed.

Appendix C. The Evolution of Cyberspace Operations

This appendix provides an overview of the history of the 17D (cyberspace operations) workforce—how cyberspace, as a domain, has matured and gained prominence since the mid-1980s—and its ongoing challenges.

In recent years there has been an increased awareness of network vulnerability and the need to invest in cybersecurity. This heightened urgency dates back to the revelation of high-profile attacks in 2007, which prompted a string of policy initiatives (Libicki, Senty, and Pollack, 2014). The DoD's *2015 DoD Cyber Strategy* uses a recent commercial example and cites North Korea's 2014 cyberattack against Sony Pictures Entertainment to demonstrate the need for strategic seriousness vis-à-vis cybersecurity (U.S. Department of Defense, 2015).

Other equally egregious examples underscore the urgency of cybersecurity and cyberspace operations, such as the 2015 cyberhack on the Office of Personnel Management and the alleged cyberattacks involving the 2016 U.S. presidential campaign. Cyberspace vulnerabilities can assume many forms, as the opening text in DoD's cyber strategy states: "We live in a wired world. Companies and countries rely on cyberspace for everything from financial transactions to the movement of military forces" (U.S. Department of Defense, 2015). Thus, while current cyberthreats have received a great deal of attention, a thorough discussion of the 17D workforce is better contextualized by revisiting what, exactly, catapulted cyberspace operations to where they now rest.

Our goal in this appendix is fourfold: (1) we explain DoD's drive to create and sustain an innovative, technologically advanced joint cybersecurity workforce; (2) we describe the unique role currently played by the Air Force in helping to protect cyberspace; (3) we show the progression of the cyberspace career field from its early stages until now; and (4) we provide a snapshot of the sentiments and descriptors used by senior leaders and airmen to describe today's 17D workforce.

Modern Developments in the DoD Cyber Workforce

The Joint Chiefs of Staff (2013) define cyberspace as

> the global domain within the information environment consisting of the interdependent network of information technology (IT) infrastructures and resident data, including the Internet, telecommunications networks, computer systems and embedded processors and controllers.

The U.S. military and its allies and partner nations leverage developments in cyberspace to maintain a "strategic and continuing advantage in the operational environment," according to

JP 3-12(R) (Joint Chiefs of Staff, 2013). It also differentiates cyber from the other four physical domains—air, space, land, and maritime—by virtue of it being man-made rather than organic.

DoD has engaged in a decades-long struggle to protect its networks and computers. Its *2015 Cyber Strategy* marries cyberspace strategic objectives to cybersecurity vulnerabilities while stressing that the internet was originally designed to be an open system whereby researchers and scientists could quickly send data to one another. As the World Wide Web came online in the early 1990s, its architects were more focused on operability than security (U.S. Department of Defense, 2015), yet vulnerabilities quickly became apparent in both the commercial and defense sectors. According to the Government Accountability Office (GAO), by the mid-1990s DoD was already heavily dependent on computer systems and their related infrastructure (U.S. Government Accountability Office, 1991). It approached the acquisition of computers and related software with a rapid intensity that was poorly coordinated (Courville, 2007). A much-needed road map for the future was missing, the lack of which resulted in deficiencies such as hardware and software weaknesses, a lack of standardization, and shortcomings in training. It was not long before the department internalized the link between protecting these systems and maintaining national security.

The GAO captured a range of these problems in its seminal report from November 1991, *Computer Security: Hackers Penetrate DoD Computer Systems*, wherein it states, "The government faces increased levels of risk for information security because of greater network use and computer literacy, and greater dependency on information technology overall." Citing the same types of statistics that are common today, it also explains

> Between April 1990 and May 1991, computer systems at 34 DoD sites attached to the Internet were successfully penetrated by foreign hackers. The hackers exploited well-known security weaknesses—many of which were exploited in the past by other hacker groups. These weaknesses persist because of inadequate attention to computer security, such as password management, and the lack of technical expertise on the part of some system administrators. (U.S. Government Accountability Office, 1991)

According to Courville, following its initial report in 1991, the GAO would eventually publish more than 50 additional reports containing the "common theme of pervasive weakness in cyber defense and security throughout government" (Courville, 2007, p. 14). Figure C.1 assembles these formative events into a time line describing the early evolution of cyber at DoD.

To be fair, security improvements have occurred despite the hypercritical cloud under which cyber operations sit, but many wonder if these changes could have been hastened early on. For example, in 1991 advocates for the cyber community lamented the lack of technical expertise and capable equipment.[1] Since then notable milestones that helped cyber gain prominence within

---

[1] As evidenced by the perspectives of the 17Ds voiced in our interviews discussed later in this report, that this view has persisted, despite an elapsed time of 26 years

Figure C.1. Key Events Influencing the Evolution of Cyber at DoD

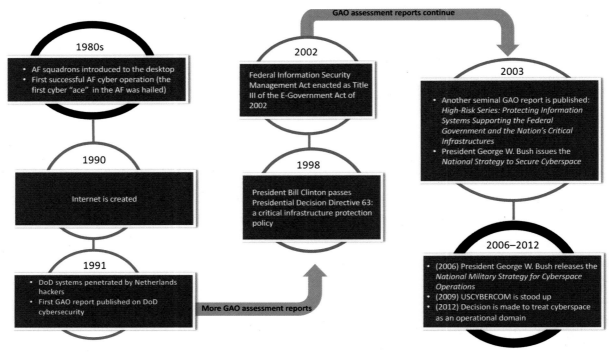

SOURCES: Courville, 2007, p. 13; Poirier and Lotspeich, 2013, p. 75; U.S. Government Accountability Office, 2003, p. 17.

DoD were the creation of U.S. Cyber Command (USCYBERCOM) in 2009 and DoD's declaration that cyberspace would be treated as an operational domain in 2011 (Healy, 2012).

These milestones were not catchall solutions to persistent operational problems; rather, they were doctrinal- and institutional-level changes that afforded the cyber community more weight and esteem. Yet a 2012 GAO report described DoD and the military services as still lacking the requisite human capital they need, stating, "In March 2011, the Commander of the U.S. Cyber Command testified that the military did not have enough highly skilled personnel to address the current and future cyber threats to our infrastructure" (U.S. Government Accountability Office, 2011). Relatedly, in his opening statement at the Senate Armed Services Committee hearing on USCYBERCOM on May 9, 2017, Sen John McCain stated,

> Threats to the United States in cyberspace continue to grow in scope and severity. But our Nation remains woefully unprepared to address these threats, which will be a defining feature of 21st century warfare. . . .
>
> In fact, this committee has adopted more than 50 provisions over the past four years focused on organizing, empowering and enabling the Department of Defense to deter and defend against threats in cyberspace.
>
> But cyber is an issue that requires an integrated whole-of-government approach. We simply do not have that now. The very fact that each agency of government believes it is responsible for defending the homeland is emblematic of our dysfunction. (U.S. Senate Committee on Armed Services, 2017)

These remarks suggest that core problems still exist across the spectrum of military services that make up DoD. During the same hearing, Senator McCain affirmed that positive strides such as the Cyber Mission Force (CMF) had borne fruit. Designed to include 6,200 military service members—in addition to civilian and contractor support personnel—the CMF planned to organize these cyber specialists into 133 Cyber Protection Teams (U.S. Department of Defense, 2015) with full operational capability by 2018.[2] In 2013, DoD described the CMF as a "major investment in its cyber personnel and technologies" (U.S. Department of Defense, 2015).

To continue making progress, DoD's *2015 Cyber Strategy* outlines five strategic goals:

1. Build and maintain ready forces and capabilities to conduct cyberspace operations.
2. Defend the DoD information network, secure DoD data, and mitigate risks to DoD missions.
3. Be prepared to defend the U.S. homeland and U.S. vital interests from disruptive or destructive cyber.
4. Build and maintain viable cyber options and plan to use those options to control conflict escalation and to shape the conflict environment at all stages.
5. Build and maintain robust international alliances and partnerships to deter shared threats and increase international security and stability.

The topics of the goals, and their accompanying implementation guidance, make clear that the strategy seeks to build up a military capability for cyber operations that can be used alongside other weapon systems. The first goal is unique in breadth in that reaching it requires the development of the workforce, operational platforms, command and control mechanisms, and assessments of operational capacity. Other goals outline the missions and partnerships that DoD seeks to engage, and the fourth goal calls for updating combat plans with how warfighters will use cyber capabilities against their targets. In all, the fact that the current strategic direction aims to build cyber into an operational community and move away from viewing it in a support role is no small change.

Based on Senator McCain's comments to the Senate Armed Services Committee, an additional problem might exist for which a solution is yet identified: determining which military service is the primary steward of the cyberspace community. Simply put, who owns cyber? And is a more optimal paradigm one that, as Senator McCain states, delivers a whole-of-government approach?

---

[2] Each military service is to contribute to the 133 Cyber Protection Teams under its individual divisions: 39 from the Air Force, 40 from the Navy, 13 from the Marine Corps, and 41 from the Army (Pomerleau, 2016). In his opening comments at the hearing, John McCain expressed optimism that the September 30, 2018, benchmark would be met. As DoD announced on October 24, 2016, "All 133 of U.S. Cyber Command's Cyber Mission Force teams achieved initial operating capability as of Oct. 21. . . . The Cyber Mission Force currently comprises about 5,000 individuals across the 133 teams. By the end of fiscal year 2018, the goal is for the force to grow to nearly 6,200 and for all 133 teams to be fully operational, officials said, adding that full operational capability is tied to a validation that all Cyber Mission Force teams are capable of operating at full mission capacity" (U.S. Department of Defense, 2016).

The Air Force Role in Cyber

Both JP 3-12(R) and Air Force Doctrine Document (AFDD) 3-12 underscore DoD support for a joint, whole-of-government approach to cyber operations. As AFDD 3-12 states,

> USCYBERSPACE fuses the Department's full spectrum of cyberspace operations and plans, coordinates, integrates, synchronizes, and conducts activities to lead day-to-day defense and protection of DoD information networks, coordinate DoD operations providing support to military missions, direct the operations and defense of specified DoD information networks, and prepare to, and when directed, conduct full spectrum military cyberspace operations. (U.S. Air Force, 2010)

Yet the Air Force has a long history of involvement in cyberspace and might consider itself a good candidate for stewardship. It also appears to bear the brunt of criticism when debates about cybersecurity and manpower arise. For example, the Air Force was singled out among the services when, in relation to the CMF, Sen McCain remarked,

> I also am concerned with the apparent lack of trained people ready to replace individuals at the conclusion of their first assignments on the Cyber Mission Force. Unfortunately, we have already heard about some puzzling issues. Specifically, out of the 127 Air Force cyber officers that completed their first tour on the Cyber Mission Force, none went back to a cyber-related job. That is unacceptable and suggests a troubling lack of focus. It should be obvious the development of a steady pipeline of new talent and the retention of the ones we have trained already is essential to the success of the Cyber Mission Force. (U.S. Senate Committee on Armed Services, 2017)

The Air Force, however, may opt for a more optimistic depiction of its cyberspace stewardship capability. As Healy (2012, p. 16) notes, "The Air Force has a longer, more distinguished heritage in the cyber domain than any other military in the world," and asks how many of today's Air Force cyberwarriors know they can trace their lineage to Air Force cyber operations in the mid-1980s. He also quotes Maj Gen Cascaino, who ran Air Force cyber units in 1996, as stating, "We don't claim [cyber] exclusively. We think we've got good ideas. We think we've got good capabilities. And we are reaching out to the other services and the joint community to offer what we have" (Healy, 2012, p. 16, brackets in the original). Others might think the special relationship between the Air Force and cyber is evidenced by the fact that the founding commander of the Joint Task Force–Computer Network Defense in 1998 was Maj Gen John "Soup" Campbell.

If we fast-forward to the present day, we see that strategically important Air Force components—such as 24 AF/AFCYBER— often assume a large burden of leadership responsibilities in joint constructs like the CMF or USCYBERCOM.[3] Figure C.2 captures some formative events in the Air Force's experience with cyber.

Figure C.2. Formative Events in the Air Force's Experience with Cyber

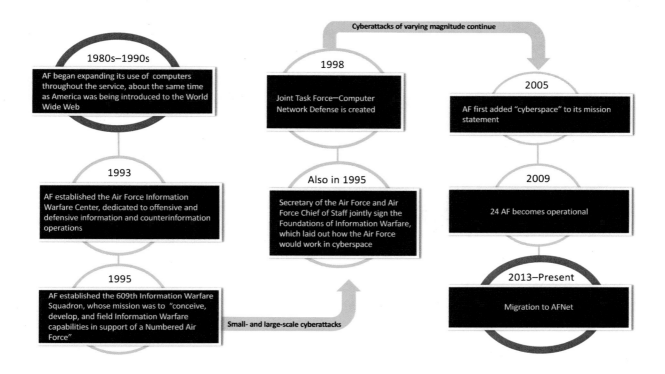

SOURCES: Courville, 2007, pp. 13–18; Healy, 2012, p. 13; Maybury, 2012, p. 68; Poirier and Lotspeich, 2013, p. 75; Vautrinot, 2012, pp. 73–77.

The Symbolism of the Air Force Network

A continuing trend in DoD cybersecurity efforts is the move to common network architectures that are easier to defend and more efficient to administer. A significant first step for the Air Force in this area was the creation of the Air Force Network (AFNet) in 2012. The impetus for creating the AFNet mirrored DoD's concerns in the 1990s—namely, that cybernetworks were too vast, disparate, and disjointed, and therefore unsafe. The seminal 1991 GAO report cited increased DoD vulnerabilities with information security due to greater network

---

[3] The 24th Air Force was established as a warfighting numbered air force focused on full-spectrum cyberspace operations (Vautrinot, 2012). AFDD 3-12 explains how 24 AF functions as the component numbered Air Force to USCYBERCOM. As such, the commander of the component numbered Air Force serves as the senior Air Force warfighter and oversees the assignment of attached forces under USCYBERCOM. AFDD 3-12 explains that USCYBERCOM comprises four service elements: 24 AF, Army Forces Cyber Command, Fleet Cyber Command, and Marine Forces Cyber Command; see U.S. Air Force (2010).

use and poor standardization across various systems. According to Courville, as the World Wide Web came into being in the 1980s and 1990s, the Air Force understood the need to integrate its computers and systems but was a far cry from working as the centralized network that "devolved into today's NIPRNeT [Nonclassified Internet Protocol Router Network]" (2007).

Computer networking was a competitive, wide-open field with multiple concepts—each with its own advantages and disadvantages—and no clear-cut consensus. As Courville notes, "The Air Force provided overarching guidance to each wing during this time period, however major commands focused on implementing networks that helped accomplish the specific mission for which each command was responsible" (2007, p. 17). The consequences were many, but the primary impact was the absence of Air Force–wide standardization over decades as the cyber domain matured. This resulted in each base managing and defending its own network. When Courville published *Air Force and the Cyberspace Mission: Defending the Air Force's Computer Network in the Future*, he dolefully described the Air Force as being a long way from providing a "robust defense with the ability to *centrally* control and defend the entire network during a cyber crisis" (2007, p. 18).

Maj Gen Suzanne M. Vautrinot, one of several proponents of greater network centralization, describes the pre-AFNet state of affairs as an outdated, manpower-intensive reactive defense posture—a heterogeneous network of legacy structures. The goal, she notes, is homogeneity and centrality for the sole purpose of security. But how do you deliver a robust, defensible, and trusted network after decades of contrary processes? Vautrinot (2012, p. 85) states,

> Armed with an understanding of the growing threat to our dependency on the network, Air Force leaders directed a service-wide migration to a more defensible network—creating the AFNet migration and facilitating a 'defense-in-depth' alignment. Helping create this defensible construct, AFSPC, through its subordinate units at 24 AF and the Air Force Network Integration Center, is reorganizing and reequipping to address the limitations resident in current Air Force heterogeneous network architecture and the underlying technologies.[4]

We began above by mentioning the disruptive effects engendered by the AFNet. Similarly disruptive were the changes made to various AFSCs, which were restructured and merged in 1986, 1993, 1996, and 2010. Many inside the Air Force were rife with opposition to both types of disruptions; with the restructuring and merging of the AFSCs came lingering and substantive impacts to the cyber career field.

---

[4] Poirier and Lotspeich (2013) reported the number of AFNet users at 850,000 in 2013.

Development of the 17D Cyber Operations Officer Career Field

Current Configuration

Cyber Mission Areas

At present, Air Force officers within the 17D cyber operations officer career field are split among three operational mission areas, the combination of which make up modern cyberwarfare: DCO, OCO, and DoDIN operations (Poirier and Lotspeich, 2013).[5] This typology is not always clearly delineated, however.

Air Force and joint force usage of the name *DoDIN* differs slightly. At the joint-force level, *DoDIN*, as a noun, refers to the global infrastructure of DoD systems covering DoD, national security, and information and intelligence from the intelligence community (Poirier and Lotspeich, 2013). Members of the Air Force 17D community, however, commonly use *DoDIN* as an adjective to describe one of the three types of cyber operators listed above. Poirier and Lotspeich (2013) describe how Air Force officers classified to perform DoDIN operations are often derided as mere IT or network support workers. A more accurate characterization, they claim, would emphasize their critical role in conducting military operations.

According to JP 3-12, DoDIN operations defend and harden a network that is a

> globally interconnected, end-to-end set of information capabilities, and associated processes for collecting, processing, sorting, disseminating, and managing information on-demand to warfighters, policy makers, and support personnel, including owned and leased communication and computer systems and services, software (including applications), data, security services, other associate services, and national security systems. (Joint Publication 3-12, 2012, quoted in Poirier and Lotspeich, 2013, p. 81)

It is often asserted that a fine line separates DoDIN operations from DCO because of the relationship between sustaining the AFNet and identifying its vulnerabilities to erect viable defenses.

The DCO mission area provides active defense to Air Force, DoD, and friendly cyberspace. For example, 24 AF DCO operators respond to enemy action by utilizing both passive and active defensive capabilities. They use a strategy called "defense in depth," which contains a set of layered, overlapping technologies. The strategy ensures monitoring and defends against access points and end points, such as clients and servers. Poirier and Lotspeich (2013, p. 82) provide additional fidelity:

> When new attacks occur that defenders could not prevent, sensors placed throughout the network supply intrusion indications and point DCO operators to the compromised systems, which they examine (by means of digital forensic

---

[5] Currently, all cyber officers are members of the 17D AFSC, regardless of whether they hold a 17D (DoDIN) or a 17S (DCO or OCO) assignment.

analysis) to determine how the intrusion occurred and what tools were used. They then develop countermeasures to prevent future attack. DCO forces remotely access forensic data from all sensor devices to counter future compromises.

The OCO mission area, according to JP 3-12(R), is designed to project power by using force in and through cyberspace: "OCO will be authorized like offensive operations in the physical domains, via an execute order (EXORD). OCO requires deconfliction in accordance with . . . current policies" (Joint Chiefs of Staff, 2013). Poirier and Lotspeich (2013, p. 85) describe how Air Force OCOs exploit an adversary's system:

> To exploit an adversary's system, offensive operations demand detailed knowledge of the target network, obtaining such information by performing network reconnaissance with sophisticated TTPs [tactics, technology, and procedures]. Once operators have identified vulnerabilities, they must then develop either a technique or a weapon or select one from an existing repository prior to choosing the specific delivery mechanism. After they have accessed their target, operators establish a permanent presence on the machine while cloaking indications of the incursion, allowing them to maintain access indefinitely.

The Cyber Squadron Initiative

The present configuration of the 17D career field is the result of a paradigm shift from viewing cyberspace as an enabler to Air Force missions to viewing it as a fully operational domain—which a recent Air Force study argues is essential for fully reaping the benefits of cyberspace (Yannakogeorgos and Geis, 2016). In order to better graft cyber forces into Air Force operations, ongoing efforts (currently denoted the Cyber Squadron Initiative) aim to transform the 17D workforce according to the organizational structure and processes that operational units use. While communications squadrons previously focused on delivering and maintaining IT services, the new direction is to leverage DoD partnerships for basic IT support to free up cyber personnel to focus on defending and securing the cyberspace used in Air Force operations (McRae, 2017). Eventually, new communications squadrons will wield mission defense teams, which are small units of trained operators that can guard cyber "terrain" as part of larger Air Force operations, and the Air Force has begun to transition units flagged as "pathfinders" to test and refine these concepts (U.S. Senate, 2017). Ultimately, the model envisions these cyber units conducting operations via the same mission planning and execution processes as other operational sectors (Collins, Chiaramonte, and McMinn, 2017).

Prior Configuration

A different taxonomy for the 17D career field existed in the not-so-distant past. The most recent change occurred in 2010, when the 33S communications and information career field was transitioned to the 17D cyber operations career field that exists today. While this was a significant change, it was not the first. In fact, the career field had undergone multiple transformations dating back to the 1980s.

Terry (2011) provides a detailed account of the vast array of changes that occurred. In 1986 the largest nonrated officer career field in the Air Force was that of 49XX, the information systems officer.

In 1993, the Air Force restructured its entire AFSC method of classification, and the information systems officer career field became the communications and computer officer career field. This was both a nominal and functional change, because after the transition this newly minted career field became so general that base-level and higher-headquarters positions were interchangeable.

In 1996 the communication and computer officer designation was involved in a triple merger whereby it was forced to absorb a total of 1,500 officers from both the 37XX information management officer and 3VXX visual information officer career fields.

Terry (2011) states, "All of the AFSCs and accompanying responsibilities that were previously spread throughout these three career fields were combined into the 33SX career field. The title for the newly organized career field officially became the Communications and Information Officer career field in recognition of the change." The functional repercussions of the merger are too numerous to discuss here, but, generally speaking, specialized expertise from the absorbed 37XX and 3VXX career fields was lost. Likewise, the prior communications and computer officer career field, while previously a highly technical field, was forced to assume many nontechnical responsibilities as a result of the merger.

As noted above, the most recent transition took place when over 3,000 officers had their 33S designation replaced with the new 17D designation. As mentioned above, 17D officers are split between DCO, OCO, and DoDIN operations. While all 17Ds receive requisite training that enables them to engage in DoDIN operations, only those that demonstrate a specific aptitude during UCT have typically been selected for DCO or OCO assignments. Similar to the restructuring that occurred in 1993, the transition from 33S to 17D in 2010 encompassed both a nominal and functional change. Functionally, the Air Force sought to "operationalize" cyber forces and create a more direct connection to warfighting. Vautrinot (2012) describes an aspect of this approach as choosing a proactive rather than reactive (defensive) orientation. This was a common theme in *Cyber Vision 2025*, in which Air Force senior leadership discussed technological, policy, and personnel changes that were needed to effectively integrate cyber with other national instruments of power. In discussing the cyberwarrior of the future, *Cyber Vision 2025* suggests more changes are coming down the pike.[6]

The mergers and transitions described above resulted in a continuous redefinition of what it meant to be a computer, communications, information systems, or cyber specialist. That

---

[6] *Cyber Vision 2025* states, "Cyber operators currently generally fall into OCO, DCO, DGO or CNE roles; future cyber operators will require the ability to seamlessly flow between these roles (and others) as the battlefield evolves and missions dictate. This will lead to changes in current organizational structures, as future mission sets evolve and stovepiped organizational structures begin to constrain operations" (Marbury, 2012, p. 68).

confusion still exists today, where officers within the career field—approximately 80 percent of whom are in DoDIN operations—struggle to find meaning and purpose given the disproportionate accolades provided to DCO and OCO officers. DoDIN officers tasked with the critical job of creating, maintaining, and sustaining the network are often exposed to messaging suggestive of their secondary status.

Concluding Thoughts

This appendix has explained the maturation of the cyberspace workforce across both DoD and the Air Force. We first profiled challenges and successes experienced by DoD because doing so shows the similar hurdles experienced by the Air Force as it worked to initiate its cyber capabilities. With both we see that early excitement over the World Wide Web and its IT offerings led to the rapid proliferation of systems, users and missions, but also opened up vulnerabilities and security weaknesses. The Air Force—which always considered itself the primary steward of cyberspace—has worked fastidiously to shore up its earlier vulnerabilities. Between 1980 and 2010 it enacted several career field modifications to produce a workable configuration of AFSCs for cyber. At present, that configuration consists of a single AFSC, 17D, but it is *conceptually* bifurcated by type of assignment held: 17D (DoDIN support and maintenance operations) versus 17S (DCO and OCO). The implications of this separation are explored extensively in this report.

Appendix D. Focus Group Questionnaire and Discussion Protocol

This appendix contains the questionnaire items provided to members of the 17D workforce who participated in focus group discussions with PAF. It also contains the discussion protocol used in the focus groups.

Questionnaire Items

1. If you were offered the opportunity to choose a cyber technical track (*meaning you could remain on keyboard over the course of your Air Force career and would not be expected to assume leadership roles*), assuming equivalent pay/benefits, how would it influence your decision regarding remaining in the active duty Air Force?

    a. Strong influence to leave
    b. Influence to leave
    c. Neither an influence to stay nor leave
    d. Influence to stay
    e. Strong influence to stay

2. If you were given the option for permeable service among the regular Air Force and Air Reserve component (*that is, to transition back and forth between RegAF and the Air National Guard or Air Force Reserve if your needs and the needs of the Air Force allowed*), would you have accepted a longer service obligation upon your initial entry into the 17D career field?

    Definitely -- Probably -- Unsure -- Probably Not -- Definitely Not

3. What best describes your current career intentions? (circle one)

    a. If provided the opportunity, definitely stay until retirement
    b. If provided the opportunity, probably stay until retirement
    c. Probably leave before I am retirement eligible
    d. Definitely leave before I am retirement eligible
    e. N/A

4. How satisfied are you with:	1 2 3 4 5 Very Neutral Very Dissatisfied Satisfied
a) your current duty assignment?	1 --- 2 --- 3 --- 4 --- 5
b) your career in general as a 17D?	1 --- 2 --- 3 --- 4 --- 5

How strongly do you agree with the following:	
5. I find real enjoyment in my work	1 2 3 4 Strongly Disagree Agree Strongly Disagree Agree

6. What do you like MOST about your job as a 17D? [Note: We cannot provide confidentiality to a participant regarding comments involving criminal activity/behavior, or statements that pose a threat to yourself or others. Do NOT discuss or comment on classified or operationally sensitive information.]

_____
_____
_____
_____
_____
_____

7. What do you like LEAST about your job as a 17D? [Note: We cannot provide confidentiality to a participant regarding comments involving criminal activity/behavior, or statements that pose a threat to yourself or others. Do NOT discuss or comment on classified or operationally sensitive information.]

_____
_____
_____
_____
_____
_____

8. What skills or qualities are critical in a 17D for ensuring mission success (or for preventing mission failure)? Why? [Note: We cannot provide confidentiality to a participant regarding comments involving criminal activity/behavior, or statements that pose a threat to yourself or others. Do NOT discuss or comment on classified or operationally sensitive information.]

_____
_____
_____
_____
_____
_____

9. Are there any other skills or qualities that 17Ds need? Why? [Note: We cannot provide confidentiality to a participant regarding comments involving criminal activity/behavior, or statements that pose a threat to yourself or others. Do NOT discuss or comment on classified or operationally sensitive information.]

_____
_____
_____
_____
_____
_____

10. How satisfied are you with the following aspects of the 17D job? (Please circle DK/NA if you don't know or the item is not applicable to you)

<u>1 2 3 4 5</u>
Very   Neutral   Very
Dissatisfied   Satisfied

a.	Military lifestyle	1 --- 2 --- 3 --- 4 --- 5	DK/NA
b.	Senior AF leadership support	1 --- 2 --- 3 --- 4 --- 5	DK/NA
c.	Senior AF leadership support for innovation	1 --- 2 --- 3 --- 4 --- 5	DK/NA
d.	Unit resources (e.g., equipment, supplies, parts, etc.)	1 --- 2 --- 3 --- 4 --- 5	DK/NA
e.	Unit readiness (i.e., mission capable status)	1 --- 2 --- 3 --- 4 --- 5	DK/NA
f.	Retention of 17Ds	1 --- 2 --- 3 --- 4 --- 5	DK/NA
g.	Resource support for innovation	1 --- 2 --- 3 --- 4 --- 5	DK/NA
h.	Quality/content of cyber IST	1 --- 2 --- 3 --- 4 --- 5	DK/NA
i.	Quality/content of cyber IQT	1 --- 2 --- 3 --- 4 --- 5	DK/NA
j.	Quality/content of cyber MQT	1 --- 2 --- 3 --- 4 --- 5	DK/NA
k.	Promotion opportunities	1 --- 2 --- 3 --- 4 --- 5	DK/NA
l.	Opportunities for career field training	1 --- 2 --- 3 --- 4 --- 5	DK/NA
m.	Opportunities for professional development	1 --- 2 --- 3 --- 4 --- 5	DK/NA
n.	Opportunities to further my academic education (noncyber focused)	1 --- 2 --- 3 --- 4 --- 5	DK/NA
o.	Opportunities to further my academic education (cyber focused)	1 --- 2 --- 3 --- 4 --- 5	DK/NA
p.	Opportunities to command/lead	1 --- 2 --- 3 --- 4 --- 5	DK/NA
q.	Job security	1 --- 2 --- 3 --- 4 --- 5	DK/NA
r.	Pay/allowances	1 --- 2 --- 3 --- 4 --- 5	DK/NA
s.	Bonuses/special pay	1 --- 2 --- 3 --- 4 --- 5	DK/NA
t.	Retirement pay	1 --- 2 --- 3 --- 4 --- 5	DK/NA
u.	Civilian job opportunities	1 --- 2 --- 3 --- 4 --- 5	DK/NA
v.	Job stress	1 --- 2 --- 3 --- 4 --- 5	DK/NA
w.	Opportunities to do special duty assignments (e.g., PME instructor, exec officer, etc.)	1 --- 2 --- 3 --- 4 --- 5	DK/NA
x.	Working in full-time duties outside of my primary specialty, excluding opportunities to do special duty assignments (e.g., PME instructor, exec officer, etc.)	1 --- 2 --- 3 --- 4 --- 5	DK/NA
y.	Ability to contribute to the mission	1 --- 2 --- 3 --- 4 --- 5	DK/NA
z.	Utilization of my skills within my unit	1 --- 2 --- 3 --- 4 --- 5	DK/NA
aa.	Recognition of my efforts	1 --- 2 --- 3 --- 4 --- 5	DK/NA

11. Suppose that you have to decide whether to stay on active duty. Assuming you could stay, how likely is it that you would choose to do so?	<u>1 2 3 4 5</u> Very Neither Very Likely Likely nor Unlikely Unlikely	DK/NA
12. How would you rate the overall quality of work done by the 17D community?	<u>1 2 3 4 5</u> Very Good / Good / Fair / Poor / Very Poor	DK/NA

95

13. Thinking about your job in the 17D cyber community, how much do you agree with the following? (Please circle DK/NA if you don't know or the item is not applicable to you)	1 2 3 4 5 Strongly Neutral Strongly Disagree Agree	
a. When short suspense/tasks arise, we do an outstanding job in handling these situations	1 --- 2 --- 3 --- 4 --- 5	DK/NA
b. 17D performance is high, compared to other AF officer career fields	1 --- 2 --- 3 --- 4 --- 5	DK/NA
c. 17D performance is high compared to private-sector cyber personnel doing work outside the military	1 --- 2 --- 3 --- 4 --- 5	DK/NA
d. The 17D community has sufficient resources (budget, equipment, technology, software, etc.) to accomplish the mission	1 --- 2 --- 3 --- 4 --- 5	DK/NA
e. The 17D community is not attracting people with the right abilities to accomplish the cyber mission	1 --- 2 --- 3 --- 4 --- 5	DK/NA
f. The 17D workforce has the job-relevant *skills* necessary to accomplish the mission	1 --- 2 --- 3 --- 4 --- 5	DK/NA
g. The 17D workforce has the job-relevant *knowledge* necessary to accomplish the mission	1 --- 2 --- 3 --- 4 --- 5	DK/NA
h. Creativity and innovation are rewarded in the 17D workforce	1 --- 2 --- 3 --- 4 --- 5	DK/NA
i. The 17D workforce is successful at accomplishing its mission	1 --- 2 --- 3 --- 4 --- 5	DK/NA
j. In my organization, senior leaders generate high levels of motivation in the workforce	1 --- 2 --- 3 --- 4 --- 5	DK/NA
k. In my organization, senior leaders generate high levels of commitment in the workforce	1 --- 2 --- 3 --- 4 --- 5	DK/NA
l. I am given a real opportunity to improve my skills in my organization	1 --- 2 --- 3 --- 4 --- 5	DK/NA
m. I feel encouraged to come up with new and better ways of doing things	1 --- 2 --- 3 --- 4 --- 5	DK/NA
n. My workload is reasonable	1 --- 2 --- 3 --- 4 --- 5	DK/NA
o. My talents are used well in the workplace	1 --- 2 --- 3 --- 4 --- 5	DK/NA
p. The work I do is important	1 --- 2 --- 3 --- 4 --- 5	DK/NA
q. I find real enjoyment in my work	1 --- 2 --- 3 --- 4 --- 5	DK/NA
r. Most days I am enthusiastic about my work	1 --- 2 --- 3 --- 4 --- 5	DK/NA
s. I like the kind of work I do	1 --- 2 --- 3 --- 4 --- 5	DK/NA
t. Training gaps exist where I've been underprepared for the jobs I've been assigned	1 --- 2 --- 3 --- 4 --- 5	DK/NA
u. AF senior leadership values the cyber mission	1 --- 2 --- 3 --- 4 --- 5	DK/NA
v. My skills/training prepared me for the responsibilities of my specialty	1 --- 2 --- 3 --- 4 --- 5	DK/NA
w. I would have difficulty finding a job if I left the military	1 --- 2 --- 3 --- 4 --- 5	DK/NA
x. Morale in my unit is good	1 --- 2 --- 3 --- 4 --- 5	DK/NA
y. I feel valued by the Air Force	1 --- 2 --- 3 --- 4 --- 5	DK/NA

14. Is there anything else important about the 17D job or quality of life that we should know about? [Note: We cannot provide confidentiality to a participant regarding comments involving criminal activity/behavior, or statements that pose a threat to yourself or others. Do NOT discuss or comment on classified or operationally sensitive information.]

_____

_____

_____

_____

_____

15. Current base location: _____

16. What is your rank? 2LT 1LT   Capt Maj Lt Col Col

17. What year did you enter as a core 17D? (NOTE: Legacy 33S AFSC counts toward entering as a core 17D) _____

18. In what year is your current service commitment up? _____

19. Are you a 17D? If no, please specify your AFSC (e.g., 14N) _____

20. Current duty AFSC? (e.g., 17D1Y, 17S3Z, C17D3Y, T17S3Y, 16G4) _____

21. Which best describes your current job specialization (circle one):

Fundamental 17D skills and activities	Cyberspace Acquisition and Program Management	Knowledge Operations Activities	Cyber Support to Intelligence Activities
Cyber Support to C3 and Battlefield Network Activities	Engineering and Installation (E&I) Activities	Cyber Support to Space Activities	Tactical Communications Activities
Combat Communications Activities	Test Squadron Activities	Cyber Contracting Activities	Cyberwarfare Operations Activities
Other, please specify: [Note: We cannot provide confidentiality to a participant regarding comments involving criminal activity/behavior, or statements that pose a threat to yourself or others. Do NOT discuss or comment on classified or operationally sensitive information.]			

22. What is your area of cyber expertise? (Mark one)

_____ Mostly OCO/DCO
_____ Mostly DoDIN ops (base comm, tactical/combat comm, E&I)
_____ Equally balanced between OCO/DCO and DoDIN ops
_____ Other (please specify which aspect of mission assurance)_____

_____

_____

23. Are you filling a special duty requirement for your career field? (e.g., PME instructor, recruiter, ROTC instructor, liaison officer, squadron officer, etc.) Yes / No

24. Are you part of a mission defense team? Yes / No

If yes, which one? _____

25. What best describes your current assignment? (Mark one)

_____ Group Level Assignment

_____ Squadron Level Assignment

_____ Wing Level Assignment

_____ Base Level Assignment

_____ Staff

_____ Other

26. Please mark the programs and/or courses you have completed:

27. _____ WIC

28. _____ CNODP

29. _____ EWI

30. _____ EWS

31. _____ RIOT

32. _____ CWO Course

33. _____ AFIT AAD (with cyber specialty)

34. _____ Intermediate Cyber Core Course

35. _____ Joint Advanced Cyber Warfare Course

36. _____ Cyber 200

37. _____ Cyber 300

38. _____ Cyberspace Officer Engineering

39. _____ Cyberspace Officer Network Training

40. _____ Cyberspace Officer Warfighting Integration Course

41. _____ Cyberspace Officer Deployable/Tactical Communications

42. _____ Enterprise Network Operations

43. _____ Joint C4I Staff and Operations Course

44. _____ Joint C4 Planners Course

45. _____ AOC Initial Qualification Training, Communications Course

46. _____ Information Operations Integration Course

47. _____ Information Operations Fundamental Applications Course

48. _____ Engineering Installations Lightning Force Academy

49. _____ AFIT School of Systems and Logistics courses (cyber focused)

50. _____ National Defense University courses (cyber focused)

51. _____ iCollege courses (cyber focused)

52. _____ CVA/Hunt Training Course

53. _____ Joint Cyberspace Operations Planners Course

54. **Please provide any additional comments here.** [Note: We cannot provide confidentiality to a participant regarding comments involving criminal activity/behavior, or statements that pose a threat to yourself or others. Do NOT discuss or comment on classified or operationally sensitive information.]

_____

_____

_____

_____

Discussion Protocol

Background

Introduction to the study, purpose, who we are, sponsor, consent overview
Icebreaker—Go around the room, list your current duty title, area of cyber expertise, total time working in cyber (5 min.).

Retention/Recruiting—Drivers and Obstacles

Drivers of attraction and retention
1. **What are the top reasons why people want to become 17Ds?**
2. **Why do you think people decide to stay a 17D once they are in the career field?**

Obstacles to retention and attraction (10 min.)
3. **What are the top reasons people don't choose to become a 17D?**
4. **Why do you think people want to leave the 17D workforce?**

Current Policy Constraints to Attracting and Retaining 17Ds

5. **What do you think the AF could do to attract or retain more or better 17Ds?**
6. OPTIONAL PROBES IF TIME AVAILABLE—How about things like:
   a. Changing the promotion/career progression requirements
   b. A technical track vs a leadership development track
   c. Separate competitive category
   d. Lateral entry
   e. Reentry
   f. Noncyber folks for FGO positions
   g. Use of civilian contractors
   h. Fitness, hair, tattoos, etc., and moral character restrictions
   i. Bonuses/incentive pays
   j. Leadership development opportunities, etc.
   k. Other force of the future initiatives
   l. Other items identified as the study proceeds

Organizational Culture, Leadership, and Other Concerns for the Career Field

7. **How many of you are satisfied you the current status and direction of the 17D career field?** Ask for a show of hands (interviewer: be sure to say the total number who agree out loud for the audio).

8. **How many of you think it needs to be improved?** (interviewer: be sure to say the total number who agree out loud for the audio). Note that people can raise their hands for both questions 7 and 8 if they want.
    a. **If so, how?**
9. **Are there other things about how the organization is structured, the existing resources, or how AF leadership treats cyber that you think need to change?**
10. **Anything else?**

Defining KSAOs

Now let's talk more about the *knowledge, skills, abilities, and expertise* that are required to do your job well. **Thinking specifically about your area of cyber expertise:**

11. **What defines a high-quality 17D?** What qualities (i.e., work experiences, education, KSAOs) are necessary for a 17D to be successful in the cyber mission (or for preventing mission failure)?
    a. Why? Give concrete examples?
    b. Ask for more qualities and examples
    c. And more
    d. (If not mentioned already) What about things like leadership?
    e. Communication?
    f. Warfighting mind-set?
    g. Anything else?

Obstacles to Getting the Right KSAOs

12. **Do you think 17D technical training and education needs to be improved/changed?** Why or why not?
    a. **How about other areas like leadership development or training in warfighting?**

Final Thoughts

13. What else should the AF be concerned about if it wants to maintain cyber capability and readiness?

14. Are there any questions you think we should have asked but didn't?

OPTIONAL ONLY IF TIME AVAILABLE

Probing for additional topics—thoughts about:

15. Civilian job opportunities
16. Pay and benefits, bonuses
17. Manning
18. Resources
19. Military lifestyle (deployments, fitness requirements, etc.)
20. Developmental opportunities (training, promotions)
21. Job stressors
22. Other things? Recognition, AF views on cyber.

Appendix E. Air Force Cyber SME Discussion Topics

This appendix contains the discussion topics used in interviews with senior Air Force SMEs in the cyber career field.

1. What defines success as a cyber operator?

   a. What knowledge, skills, abilities, and other characteristics (KSAOs) are you hoping to see in Air Force cyber personnel? What behaviors are you hoping they will exhibit?

   b. Are there differences in the required KSAOs and responsibilities between the civilian and military cyber workforce?

   c. What are examples of poor performance? What behaviors and KSAOs are you hoping to avoid?

   d. In what KSAO areas is the current workforce strong? In what areas is it lacking?

   e. Are there gaps in people's cyber abilities that are not being adequately addressed in training?

2. What are the perceived challenges to finding successful operators (training attrition, attraction and retention problems, etc.)?

   a. Are people with the right KSAOs attracted to cyber jobs in the Air Force? If not, why?

   b. Are there policies in place that prevent the Air Force from attracting or retaining successful cyber personnel?

   c. What might attract more or better people to the cyber community?

3. Recruiting and retention challenges

   a. Are recruiting or retention challenges impacting the success of the cyber mission? If so, how?

4. Leadership and culture

   a. Are there any leadership, culture, or other organizational issues impacting the success of or retention of cyber personnel? If so, in what ways?

5. Training and career progression

   a. Is the training relevant and appropriate to the demands of cyber jobs?

   b. At which points in the training do people fail at high rates? Why do they fail? Are there ways to reduce the rates of failure (either through screening or changes to the training curriculum) and still produce successful cyber operators?

   c. Are there career progression challenges in the cyber community?

6. Are there any other obstacles to success within the cyber community that we have not discussed?

Appendix F. Private-Sector Interview Questions

This appendix contains the questions used in interviews with participants from the private sector.

Choosing Cyber Jobs

1. What are the most important factors you would consider when deciding what company or organization to work for (e.g., pay, location, benefits, etc.)? What about others in the U.S. cyber workforce?

2. If you have moved from one cyber position to another, what were the most important factors when deciding to move? What do most people in the U.S cyber workforce consider when deciding to switch jobs?

3. What knowledge, skills, abilities, and other characteristics (KSAOs) do you think it takes to be a successful cyber operator in the civilian industry?

   a. How do individuals develop those KSAOs?

   b. How do companies find individuals with those KSAOs?

Questions about the Air Force

4. What are your general perceptions of the U.S. Air Force, both in terms of what it does and the people who join it?

   a. What do you think draws a person to join the Air Force?

5. What are your general perceptions of the military's cyber operation capabilities? Example follow-up questions depending on response/time:

   a. When you think of the military performing cyber operations, what do you think they do?

   b. Do you think highly of the work they do?

   c. Do you think they have up-to-date technologies?

   d. Do you think they are supported by their leadership?

   e. Are you aware of the different types of cyber jobs in the Air Force?

6. Recruiting and Retention Recommendations

   a. What do you think the best way is for the Air Force to recruit individuals who are interested in cyber and have the necessary KSAOs? What would make an AF job attractive to you or others in the U.S. cyber workforce?

   b. What types of things would help retain them? What would make them leave?

   c. Are there things you attribute to military service (e.g., fitness standards, uniform/grooming requirements, mobility) that may detract from cyber personnel joining/staying?

References

Air Force Personnel Center, *Air Force Officer Classification Directory (AFOCD): The Official Guide to the Air Force Officer Classification Codes*, OPR: HQ AFPC/DP3DW, October 31, 2017. As of July 3, 2018:
http://www.afpc.af.mil/Portals/70/documents/07_CLASSIFICATION/Air%20Force%20Officer%20Classification%20Directory_Oct2017.pdf?ver=2018-02-28-085253-070

Bagchi-Sen, Sharmistha, H. R. Rao, and Shambhu J. Upadhyaya, "Women in Cybersecurity: A Study of Career Advancement," *IT Professional*, Vol. 12, No. 1, 2010, pp. 24–31.

Brouse, Peggy, "Systems Engineering in a Cyber Security Engineering Program," *INCOSE International Symposium*, Vol. 25, No. 1, 2015, pp. 1403–1416. As of July 4, 2018:
http://dx.doi.org/10.1002/j.2334-5837.2015.00138.x

Campbell, Susan G., Polly O'Rourke, and Michael F. Bunting, "Identifying Dimensions of Cyber Aptitude," *Proceedings of the Human Factors and Ergonomics Society Annual Meeting*, Vol. 59, No. 1, 2015, pp. 721–725.

Carretta, Thomas R., "Pilot Candidate Selection Method: Still an Effective Predictor of US Air Force Pilot Training Performance," *Aviation Psychology and Applied Human Factors*, Vol. 1, No. 1, 2011, pp. 3–8.

Chappelle, Wayne, Kent McDonald, James Christensen, Lillian Prince, Tanya Goodman, William Thompson, and William Hayes, *Sources of Occupational Stress and Prevalence of Burnout and Clinical Distress Among U.S. Air Force Cyber Warfare Operators*, Wright-Patterson Air Force Base, Ohio: Air Force Research Laboratory, 2013.

Collins, Jeffrey A., Michael V. Chiaramonte, and Lucille R. McMinn, *Functional Mission Analysis for the Air Force Cyber Squadron Initiative*, Air Force CyberWorx Report 17-001, Colorado Springs, Colo.: U.S. Air Force Academy, Office of Scientific Research, March 17, 2017. As of July 4, 2018:
http://www.dtic.mil/dtic/tr/fulltext/u2/1032933.pdf

Conti, Gregory, and David Raymond, "Leadership of Cyber Warriors: Enduring Principles and New Directions," *Small Wars Journal*, July 2011. As of July 4, 2018:
http://smallwarsjournal.com/blog/journal/docs-temp/811-contiraymond.pdf

Courville, Shane P., "Air Force and the Cyberspace Mission Defending the Air Force's Computer Network in the Future," Maxwell Air Force Base, Ala.: Center for Strategy and Technology, Air War College, 2007.

Evans, Karen, and Franklin Reeder, "A Human Capital Crisis in Cybersecurity: Technical Proficiency Matters," Washington, D.C.: Center for Strategic and International Studies, Commission on Cybersecurity for the 44th Presidency, November 2010.

Griffeth, Rodger W., Peter W. Hom, and Stefan Gaertner, "A Meta-Analysis of Antecedents and Correlates of Employee Turnover: Update, Moderator Tests, and Research Implications for the Next Millennium," *Journal of Management*, Vol. 26, No. 3, 2000, pp. 463–488.

Hanser, Lawrence M., Nelson Lim, Douglas Yeung, and Eric Cring, *Improving Development Teams to Support Deliberate Development of Air Force Officers*, Santa Monica, Calif.: RAND Corporation, RR-1010-AF, 2015. As of July 4, 2018:
https://www.rand.org/pubs/research_reports/RR1010.html

Hardison, Chaitra, Eyal Aharoni, Christopher Larson, Steven Trochlil, and Alexander C. Hou, *Stress and Dissatisfaction in the Air Force's Remotely Piloted Aircraft Community: Focus Group Findings*, Santa Monica, Calif.: RAND Corporation, RR-1756-AF, 2017. As of August 22, 2017:
https://www.rand.org/pubs/research_reports/RR1756.html

Healy, Jason, "Claiming the Lost Cyber Heritage," *Strategic Studies Quarterly*, Vol. 6, No. 3, Fall 2012, pp. 11–19.

Hosek, James, Michael G. Mattock, C. Christine Fair, Jennifer Kavanagh, Jennifer Sharp, and Mark E. Totten, *Attracting the Best: How the Military Competes for Information Technology Personnel*, Santa Monica, Calif.: RAND Corporation, MG-108-OSD, 2004. As of September 20, 2017:
https://www.rand.org/pubs/monographs/MG108.html

Jabbour, Kamal, *CyberVision and Cyber Force Development*, Maxwell Air Force Base, Ala.: Air University, 2010.

Joint Chiefs of Staff, *Cyberspace Operations*, Joint Publication 3-12(R), Washington D.C.: U.S. Department of Defense, February 5, 2013. As of July 4, 2018:
https://www.hsdl.org/?view&did=758858

Kristof-Brown, Amy L., Ryan D. Zimmerman, and Erin C. Johnson, "Consequences of Individuals' Fit at Work: A Meta-Analysis of Person-Job, Person-Organization, Person-Group, and Person-Supervisor Fit," *Personnel Psychology*, Vol. 58, No. 2, 2005, pp. 281–342.

Langley, John, *Occupational Burnout and Retention of Air Force Distributed Common Ground System (DCGS) Intelligence Personnel*, Santa Monica, Calif.: RAND Corporation, RGSD-306, 2012. As of August 22, 2017:
https://www.rand.org/pubs/rgs_dissertations/RGSD306.html

LeClair, Jane, Sherly Abraham, and Lifang Shih, "An Interdisciplinary Approach to Educating an Effective Cyber Security Workforce," *Proceedings of the 2013 on InfoSecCD '13: Information Security Curriculum Development Conference*, New York, N.Y.: Association for Computing Machinery, 2013. As of July 5, 2018:
http://dl.acm.org/citation.cfm?doid=2528908.2528923

LeClair, Jane, Lifang Shih, and Sherly Abraham, "Women in STEM and Cyber Security Fields," paper presented at the Conference for Industry and Education Collaboration, Savannah, Ga., February 2014.

Libicki, Martin C., David Senty, and Julia Pollak, *Hackers Wanted: An Examination of the Cybersecurity Labor Market*, Santa Monica, Calif.: RAND Corporation, RR-430, 2014. As of July 5, 2018:
http://www.rand.org/pubs/research_reports/RR430.html

Mattock, Michael G., and Jeremy Arkes, *The Dynamic Retention Model for Air Force Officers: New Estimates and Policy Simulations of the Aviator Continuation Pay Program*, Santa Monica, Calif.: RAND Corporation, TR-470-AF, 2007. As of August 22, 2017:
https://www.rand.org/pubs/technical_reports/TR470.html

Mattock, Michael G., James Hosek, Beth J. Asch, and Rita Karam, *Retaining U.S. Air Force Pilots When the Civilian Demand for Pilots Is Growing*, Santa Monica, Calif.: RAND Corporation, RR-1455-AF, 2016. As of September 11, 2017:
https://www.rand.org/pubs/research_reports/RR1455.html

Maybury, Mark T., *Cyber Vision 2025: United States Air Force Cyberspace Science and Technology Vision, 2012–2025*, AF/ST TR 12-01, Washington, D.C.: U.S. Air Force, Office of the Chief Scientist, 2012. As of September 20, 2017:
https://www.globalsecurity.org/security/library/policy/usaf/cybervision2025_afd-130327 -306.pdf

McRae, Jannelle, "Cyber Squadron Initiative: Arming Airmen for the 21st Century Battle," May 5, 2017. As of September 21, 2017:
http://www.af.mil/News/Article-Display/Article/1174583/cyber-squadron-initiative-arming -airmen-for-21st-century-battle/

Moix, Cameron, "USAFA: CyberWorx Program Is Now Operational," *Colorado Springs Business Journal*, February 17, 2017. As of September 12, 2017:
www.csbj.com/2017/02/17/usafa-cyberworx-program-is-now-operational/

Morgeson, Frederick P., and Erich C. Dierdorff, "Work Analysis: From Technique to Theory," in Sheldon Zedeck, ed., *APA Handbook of Industrial and Organizational Psychology*: Vol. 2, *Selecting and Developing Members for the Organization*, Washington, D.C.: American Psychological Association, 2011, pp. 3–41.

National Research Council, *Professionalizing the Nation's Cybersecurity Workforce? Criteria for Decision-Making*. Washington, D.C.: National Academies Press, 2013. As of July 5, 2018: https://doi.org/10.17226/18446

Poirier, William J., and James Lotspeich, "Air Force Cyber Warfare: Now and the Future," *Air & Space Power Journal*, Vol. 27, No. 5, September–October 2013, pp. 73–97. As of July 5, 2018: http://www.airuniversity.af.mil/Portals/10/ASPJ/journals/Volume-27_Issue-5/ F-Poirier_Lotspeich.pdf

Pomerleau, Mark, "DoD's Long Path to Creating a Cyber Warrior Workforce," Defense Systems, March 4, 2016. As of September 20, 2017: https://defensesystems.com/Articles/2016/03/04/DoD-cyber-warrior-workforce.aspx?Page=2

Raytheon, *Preparing Millennials to Lead in Cyberspace*, Sterling, Va.: Raytheon, October 2014. As of July 3, 2018: https://www.raytheon.com/news/rtnwcm/groups/gallery/documents/digitalasset/rtn_210603.pdf

Schmidt, Lara, Caolionn O'Connell, Hirokazu Miyake, Akhil R. Shah, Joshua Baron, Geof Nieboer, Rose Jourdan, David Senty, Zev Winkelman, Louise Taggart, Susanne Sondergaard, and Neil Robinson, *Cyber Practices: What Can the U.S. Air Force Learn from the Commercial Sector?* Santa Monica, Calif.: RAND Corporation, RR-847-AF, 2015. As of August 22, 2017: https://www.rand.org/pubs/research_reports/RR847.html

Schneider, Benjamin, Harold W. Goldstein, and D. Brent Smith, "The ASA Framework: An Update," *Personnel Psychology*, Vol. 48, No. 4, 1995, pp. 747–773.

Scott, Lynn, Ray Conley, Richard Mesic, Edward O'Connell, and Darren D. Medlin, *Human Capital Management for the USAF Cyber Force*, Santa Monica, Calif.: RAND Corporation, DB-579-AF, 2010. As of August 22, 2017: https://www.rand.org/pubs/documented_briefings/DB579.html

Secretary of the Air Force Public Affairs, "Air Force Announces 100 Percent Promotion Opportunity to Major," September 14, 2017. As of July 5, 2018: http://www.afpc.af.mil/News/Article-Display/Article/1309786/air-force-announces -100-percent-promotion-opportunity-to-major/

Suby, Michael, *The 2015 (ISC)² Global Information Security Workforce Study*, San Antonio, Tex.: Frost & Sullivan, 2015.

Terry, Katrina A., "Overcoming the Support Focus of the 17D Cyberspace Operations Career Field," Wright-Patterson Air Force Base, Ohio: Air University, Air Force Institute of Technology, 2011. As of 25 August 2017: http://www.dtic.mil/dtic/tr/fulltext/u2/a545792.pdf

Trippe, D. Matthew, Karen O. Moriarty, Teresa L. Russell, Thomas R. Carretta, and Adam S. Beatty, "Development of a Cyber/Information Technology Knowledge Test for Military Enlisted Technical Training Qualification," *Military Psychology*, Vol. 26, No. 3, 2014, pp. 182–198.

U.S. Air Force, *Cyberspace Operations*, Air Force Doctrine Document 3-12, July 15, 2010. As of July 4, 2018:
https://nsarchive2.gwu.edu/NSAEBB/NSAEBB424/docs/Cyber-060.pdf

———, *Core Doctrine:* Vol. 2, *Leadership*, August 8, 2015. As of February 18, 2018:
http://www.doctrine.af.mil/Portals/61/documents/Volume_2/Volume-2-Leadership.pdf?ver=2017-09-17-123840-740

———, *Air Force Instruction AFI36-2101: Active Duty Service Commitments (ADSC)*, March 8, 2017. As of February 18, 2018:
http://static.e-publishing.af.mil/production/1/af_a1/publication/afi36-2101/afi36-2101.pdf

U.S. Department of Defense, *Department of Defense Cyberspace Workforce Strategy*, Washington D.C.: U.S. Department of Defense, December 4, 2013. As of September 12, 2017:
http://dodcio.defense.gov/Portals/0/Documents/DoD%20Cyberspace%20Workforce%20Strategy_signed%28final%29.pdf

———, *The DoD Cyber Strategy*, Washington D.C.: U.S. Department of Defense, 2015. As of September 20, 2017:
https://www.defense.gov/Portals/1/features/2015/0415_cyber-strategy/Final_2015_DoD_CYBER_STRATEGY_for_web.pdf

———, "All Cyber Mission Force Teams Achieve Initial Operating Capability," U.S. Department of Defense, October 24, 2016. As of September 20, 2017:
https://www.defense.gov/News/Article/Article/984663/all-cyber-mission-force-teams-achieve-initial-operating-capability/

U.S. Government Accountability Office, *Computer Security: Hackers Penetrate DoD Computer Systems*, GAO/T-IMTEC-92-5, Washington, D.C.: U.S. Government Accountability Office, 1991. As of August 23, 2017:
http://www.gao.gov/assets/110/104234.pdf

———, *Information Security: Further Efforts Needed to Fully Implement Statutory Requirements in DoD*, GAO-03-1037T, Washington, D.C.: U.S. Government Accountability Office, July 2003.

———, *Cybersecurity Human Capital: Initiatives Need Better Planning and Coordination*, GAO-12-8, Washington, D.C.: U.S. Government Accountability Office, 2011. As of July 4, 2018:
https://www.gao.gov/assets/590/586494.pdf

U.S. House of Representatives, *Military Pilot Shortage: Hearings Before the Subcommittee on Military Personnel, Committee on Armed Services*, Washington, D.C.: U.S. Government Printing Office, 2017.

U.S. Senate, *Military Cyber Programs and Posture: Hearings Before the Subcommittee on Cybersecurity*, United States Senates Committee on Armed Services: Washington, D.C., 2017.

U.S. Senate Committee on Armed Services, *Hearing to Receive Testimony on United States Cyber Command*, 2017. As of September 20, 2017:
https://www.armed-services.senate.gov/imo/media/doc/17-42_05-09-17.pdf

Vautrinot, Suzanne M., "Sharing the Cyber Journey," *Strategic Studies Quarterly*, Vol. 6, No. 3, 2012, pp. 71–87. As of July 4, 2018:
http://www.airuniversity.af.mil/Portals/10/SSQ/documents/Volume-06_Issue-3/Vautrinot.pdf

Vogel, Rebecca, "Closing the Cybersecurity Skills Gap," *Salus Journal*, Vol. 4, No. 2, 2016, pp. 32–46.

Waage, Erick, and Jeffrey Morris, "Cyber Aptitude Assessment: Finding the Next Generation of Enlisted Cyber Soldiers," *Cyber Defense Review*, Vol. 2, No. 3, November 16, 2015. As of July 5, 2018:
https://cyberdefensereview.army.mil/The-Journal/Article-Display/Article/1136034/cyber-aptitude-assessment-finding-the-next-generation-of-enlisted-cyber-soldiers/

Wenger, Jennie W., Caolionn O'Connell, and Maria C. Lytell, *Retaining the Army's Cyber Expertise*, Santa Monica, Calif.: RAND Corporation, RR-1978-A, 2017. As of September 26, 2017:
https://www.rand.org/pubs/research_reports/RR1978.html

Westermeyer, Roger H., *Recruiting and Retaining Cyberwarriors*, Carlisle, Pa.: U.S. Army War College, 2008.

Yannakogeorgos, Panayotis A., and John Geis II. *The Human Side of Cyber Conflict: Organizing, Training, and Equipping the Air Force Cyber Workforce*, Maxwell Air Force Base, Ala.: Air Force Research Institute, 2016.